A Step-by-Step Guide to Motoring Law

Callow Publishing

A Step-by-Step Guide to Motoring Law

by Neil Corre, LL.B, Solicitor

London
Callow Publishing
1996

ISBN 1 898899 10 X

All rights reserved

Every care is taken in the preparation of this publication, but the author, publishers and distributors cannot accept responsibility for the consequences of any error, however caused.

© 1996, N Corre

Published by Callow Publishing Limited,
133 Upper Street, London N1 1QP
Distributed by Springfield Books Ltd, Norman Road, Denby Dale,
Huddersfield HD8 8TH. Tel: (01484) 864955. FAX: (01484) 865443
Printed and bound in Great Britain by
Hartnolls Limited, Bodmin, Cornwall

In memory of my father

Preface

Motoring law is too important to be left to lawyers. Every time you use your car you are entering a legal minefield. You must have a valid driving licence, road fund licence and insurance. Tyres, brakes and steering gear must be in good and efficient working order. Wipers, lighting equipment, reflectors, silencers and seat belts must comply with legal requirements. You must obey traffic signs, parking and waiting restrictions and pedestrian crossing regulations. You must not obstruct the highway or leave a vehicle in a dangerous position. You must not exceed the speed limit or drive dangerously, carelessly or under the influence of drink or drugs.

A great many motorists have insufficient regard to these requirements. In 1993, the police took action on 7 million traffic offences, and 2.4 million of these offences were dealt with by the courts. For many motorists, breach of the law has severe consequences; 182,000 were disqualified from driving in 1993, 41 per cent of them for more than one year.

In 1994, 3,651 people were killed on the roads, the lowest figure since records began in 1926, despite the increase in motor vehicles and mileage travelled. This is partly due to improvements in vehicle design and medical science but it is also due to a change in public attitudes to driving, particularly to drink driving, to which one in five road deaths is attributed.

Research shows that the public regards drink driving as five times more serious than shoplifting and twice as serious as the burglary of an empty house. Public information campaigns against drink driving both reflect and influence this attitude. The "Think Before your Drink and Drive" and "Don't Drink and Drive – You Know it Makes Sense" slogans of the 1960s gave way to "What Should You Call People who Slaughter 1100 a year?" and "If you Drink and Drive, You're a Menace to Society" in the 1980s and "Drinking and Driving Wrecks Lives" in the 1990s. A Department of Transport campaign in 1995 to label drink drivers "murderers" was abandoned only after protests from the Home Office, but the television advertisements were considered so disturbing that they could be shown only after the 9 pm watershed.

Public awareness of the dangers of excess speed is growing. The Department of Transport estimates that excess speed is responsible for 1,000 deaths and 77,000 injuries a year. It is anomalous that the law prohibits driving in excess of 70 m.p.h., but there are no legal restrictions on the production and marketing of vehicles capable of exceeding the speed limit. A possible solution is to fit vehicles with automatic speed limiters. The technology also exists for the production of speed disclosers which could be fitted to the outside of a vehicle to show a given colour when the vehicle is travelling in excess of the speed limit. The political will to require such devices has not been forthcoming.

The purpose of this book is twofold: (1) to set out the law in a way which is intelligible to the non-lawyer so that he or she can avoid the pitfalls of motoring law; (2) to provide sufficient information to a motorist who is facing legal proceedings to decide whether or not there is a defence to the charge and, if not, how to seek a penalty towards the lower end of the relevant scale.

This book cannot be a substitute for the detailed advice you will obtain from a solicitor who knows the particular circumstances of your case. It is intended to provide sufficient information to enable you to deal with a routine case without legal representation and to enable you to make an informed decision as to whether more detailed advice is needed in your particular case.

For many people a court appearance can be a distressing and traumatic experience. If this book helps the reader to avoid that experience, or advance a defence that is appropriate, or to argue successfully for a modest penalty, then it will have achieved its aim.

Thanks are due to Mr Graham Fillingham, and to Ms Nikki Barr, who read the proofs.

Tribute must also be paid to my wife Corinne and sons Stefan and Adam for providing sufficient refreshment for my blood-tea level to exceed the prescribed limit while writing this book.

Happy Motoring!

Contents

Chapter 1: Introduction, 13
The powers of the police, 13
Terminology used in motoring law, 16
Terminology used in court proceedings, 20
Terminology used in sentencing, 25
The magistrates' court and its personnel, 27
An outline of magistrates' court procedure, 28

Chapter 2: Documents, 36
Introduction, 36
Producing documents, 36
Failure to produce documents, 37
Using an uninsured vehicle, 37
Using a motor vehicle without a test certificate, 38
Driving otherwise than in accordance with a driving licence, 39
Driving after refusal or revocation of licence, 40
Using or keeping a vehicle without an excise licence, 41
Failing to display an excise licence, 42

Chapter 3: Standards of driving, 43
Driving without due care and attention, 43
Driving without reasonable consideration, 45
Dangerous driving, 45
Causing death by dangerous driving, 48
Motor manslaughter, 49
Wanton or furious driving, 50
Motor racing, 50

Chapter 4: Speeding, 52
Types of speeding offence, 52
Exceeding the speed limit on a restricted road, 52

A Step-by-Step Guide to Motoring Law

                Exceeding a temporary limit or restriction on roads other than motorways, 53
                Exceeding the limit applicable to a particular class of vehicle, 54
                Exceeding the limit imposed by a local authority, 54
                Exceeding the limit on a motorway, 55
                Exemption for the fire brigade, police and ambulance service, 55
                Evidence, 55
                Penalties, 56

Chapter 5:   **Motorways, 57**
                Introduction, 57
                Driving otherwise than on a carriageway, 57
                Driving in the wrong direction, 58
                U-turns, 58
                Stopping, 58
                Reversing, 59
                Using the central reservation or verge, 59
                Learner drivers, 59
                The right hand lane, 59
                Animals, 60
                Excluded traffic, 60
                Pedestrians, 60
                General defences, 60
                Penalties, 61

Chapter 6:   **Construction and Use, 62**
                Introduction, 62
                Using a vehicle in a dangerous condition, 62
                Tyres, 64
                Brakes, 65
                Steering gear, 65
                Strict liability, 65
                Penalties, 65
                The vehicle defect rectification scheme, 66

Chapter 7:   **Accidents, 67**
                Introduction, 67
                Failing to stop after an accident, 67
                Failing to report an accident, 67
                Failing to produce an insurance certificate following a

A Step-by-Step Guide to Motoring Law

                personal injury accident, 68
            Defence, 68
            Penalties, 68

Chapter 8: **Traffic Directions and Traffic Signs, 70**
            Failing to comply with a direction given by a constable, 70
            Failure to comply with a traffic sign, 70

Chapter 9: **Pedestrian Crossings, 74**
            Zebra crossings, 74
            Pelican crossings, 74
            Failure to accord precedence on a zebra crossing, 75
            Stopping in a zebra-controlled area, 75
            Overtaking in a zebra-controlled area, 75
            Failure to accord precedence on a pelican crossing, 76
            Stopping in an area adjacent to a pelican crossing, 76
            Defences, 76

Chapter 10: **Seat Belts and Protective Headgear, 78**
            Introduction, 78
            Seat belts, 78
            Protective headgear, 80

Chapter 11: **Parking, 82**
            Local orders, 82
            Wheel clamping, 83
            Penalty charge notices (parking tickets), 84
            Endorsable parking offences, 85
            Opening the door of a motor vehicle, 86

Chapter 12: **Criminal Offences, 88**
            Introduction, 88
            Taking a conveyance, 88
            Aggravated vehicle taking, 91
            Interfering with a motor vehicle, 92
            Driving whilst disqualified, 93
            Obtaining a driving licence while disqualified, 94
            After the disqualification period, 94
            Fraudulent use of a vehicle excise licence, 94
            Causing danger to road users, 95

A Step-by-Step Guide to Motoring Law

Chapter 13: Alcohol and Drugs, 97
Introduction, 97
An outline of the drink-drive law, 99
Powers of arrest, 100
Powers of entry, 101
The screening or preliminary or roadside breath test, 101
Driving or attempting to drive with excess alcohol, 102
Driving whilst unfit, 106
In charge whilst unfit or with excess alcohol, 107
Special protection for a hospital patient, 108
Failing to provide a specimen, 108
Disqualification, 110
Causing death by careless driving when under the influence of drink or drugs, 112
Penalties, 113
Removal or reduction of period of disqualification, 115
Operating principles of the breath analysis machines, 116

Chapter 14: Penalties, 118
Penalties available to the court, 118
Fixed penalty notices, 121
Endorsement and the penalty points system, 125
Disqualification, 126
Special reasons, 128
Mitigation, 130
List of imprisonable offences, 131
List of endorsable offences, 131
List of offences leading to obligatory disqualification, 132
List of fixed penalty offences, 132

Index, 135

Chapter 1

Introduction

An appearance in court can be a stressful experience. Much of the stress results from unfamiliarity with police powers, legal terminology and court procedure. This chapter is intended to put the reader at ease by giving an indication of what to expect. We shall therefore examine:
- the powers of the police;
- terminology used in motoring law;
- terminology used in court proceedings;
- the magistrates' court and its personnel;
- magistrates' court procedure, in outline.

The Powers of the Police

Power to Stop Vehicles

A police officer in uniform has a general power to stop a person driving a "mechanically propelled vehicle" or a cycle on a road. A "mechanically propelled vehicle" includes a motor car, motor cycle or van; see page 18. Failure to stop when required to do so is an offence punishable with a fine up to Level 3 on the standard scale. The standard scale of penalties, and the various levels, are explained on page 26.

Power to Stop and Search Vehicles

A police officer may stop and search a vehicle if he has reasonable grounds for suspecting that he will find in it stolen goods, or a prohibited article such as an offensive weapon.

Road Checks

A police officer may conduct a road check to ascertain whether a

vehicle is carrying:
- a person who has committed a "serious arrestable offence" (see page 22) other than a road traffic offence or a vehicle excise licence offence;
- a person who is a witness to such an offence;
- a person intending to commit such an offence;
- a person who is unlawfully at large, such as an escaped prisoner.

Power of Arrest

A police officer may arrest without warrant anyone whom he has reasonable grounds for suspecting to be guilty of what is known as an "arrestable offence" (see page 22). The arrestable offences dealt with in this book are causing death by dangerous driving (see page 48); causing death by careless driving when under the influence of drink or drugs (page 112); manslaughter (page 49); causing danger to road users (see page 95); taking a conveyance (see page 88) and aggravated taking (see page 91).

Certain other offences dealt with in this book also carry a power of arrest without a warrant, and these are:
- all the offences mentioned in Chapter 13 (alcohol and drug-related offences);
- interfering with a motor vehicle;
- driving whilst disqualified.

The other offences dealt with in this book do not carry a power of arrest, and a person suspected of committing one of them will usually be sent a summons (see page 20). The police may, however, arrest for a non-arrestable offence where service of a summons would be inappropriate or impracticable, for example because the person gave a false name or address or refused to give a name and address.

If proceedings are brought against a person who is arrested, the person will be the subject of a charge (see page 21) rather than of a summons.

Power to Detain

A person who has been arrested may be detained for up to 24 hours (the period may be extended in certain extreme circumstances) before being charged. While in police detention, a person has a right to have a friend or relation informed of his arrest and to have access to legal advice.

A person who is in police detention may be questioned by the police, and although the person does not have to answer the questions, it may harm his or her defence not to mention, when questioned, something which he or she later relies on in court.

If you are arrested and the police wish to question you, you should avail yourself of your right to legal advice. If you do not know a solicitor, you should ask for the duty solicitor, whose advice is free and independent of the police.

Power to Issue a Prohibition Notice

A prohibition notice is a notice issued by a police officer which prohibits the driving of a defective vehicle if driving it would give rise to a danger of injury to any person; for example, a vehicle with no brakes.

Power to Obtain the Name and Address of a Driver

The police have power to require a driver to give his or her name and address and the name and address of the owner of the vehicle, whether or not the driver is suspected of an offence, and whether or not there has been an accident.

Power to Require Production of Documents

The police have power to require a driver to produce a certificate of insurance, test certificate and driving licence. If these documents are not in the driver's possession at the time, the police officer will issue to the driver a form "HORT 1" (also known as a "notice to produce"), requiring the documents to be produced at a police station of the driver's choice within seven days. If you are involved in an accident where personal injury is caused, you must produce your certificate of insurance to a police station within seven days.

Power to Require Information as to Identity of Driver

Where the driver of a motor vehicle is suspected of an offence:
- the keeper of the vehicle (that is, the person who is registered as the keeper by the Driver and Vehicle Licensing Authority in Swansea) must give information as to the identity of the driver

Introduction

when required to do so by or on behalf of the police, and
- any other person, and this can include the driver of the vehicle, must, if required, give any information which is in that person's power to give which may lead to the identity of the driver.

If a person is charged with the offence of failing to give such information, it is a defence to prove:
- that he or she was not the driver; or
- that it is not in his or her power to give the information; or
- that he or she did not know, and could not with reasonable diligence have ascertained, who the driver was.

The offence is subject to a fine up to Level 3 on the standard scale, obligatory endorsement with 3 penalty points (unless committed by a company) and discretionary disqualification (unless committed by a company). Endorsement and disqualification are explained in Chapter 14.

Power to Require the Removal of Vehicles

A police officer may require the owner or driver, or other person in control or in charge, of a vehicle to move the vehicle if it has broken down or has been left on a road so as to cause an obstruction or danger to persons using the road, or if it is there in breach of a traffic prohibition or restriction.

For the meaning of "in charge", see page 107. "In control" has a wider meaning and extends to vehicles controlled by pedestrians, such as a lawn mower. It also includes persons such as driving instructors who are in control of a vehicle but not necessarily in charge of it.

Power to Remove Vehicles

A police officer may remove a vehicle which has broken down or has been left on a road or on any land in the open air and which appears to the officer to have been abandoned.

Similar powers rest with local authorities and traffic wardens, except that the power of a traffic warden relates to vehicles on a road only.

Terminology Used in Motoring Law

Everyday words such as "driving" and "road" are legally defined in a way that is not always apparent to the ordinary motorist. The legal meanings of such words are examined in this section.

Driving

"Driving" means using the vehicle's controls for the purpose of directing the movement of the vehicle. A person may be driving even if the vehicle is not moving under its own power, for example if it is rolling downhill or being pushed.

In a decided case, a front seat passenger, who saw a friend walking on the pavement, decided to frighten the friend by grabbing the steering wheel and pulling the car towards him. The court decided that he was not driving, but interfering with the driving.

Attempting to Drive

"Attempting to drive" means sitting in the driver's seat, either attempting to start the vehicle or attempting to put it in gear, or attempting to accelerate the engine so as to make the vehicle go forward.

Motor Cycle

A motor cycle is a mechanically propelled vehicle, not being an invalid carriage, with fewer than four wheels and whose unladen weight does not exceed 410 kilograms.

Motor Vehicle

This means a mechanically propelled vehicle intended or adapted for use on the road. Defective vehicles remain motor vehicles unless there is no realistic prospect of their being used on the road again.

Whether a vehicle is intended for use on the road does not depend on the intention of the driver in question or the intention of the manufacturer. The test is whether a reasonable person would say that the particular vehicle might well be used on the road. Applying this test:
- mechanical dumpers are not intended or adapted for use on the road and are therefore not motor vehicles;
- motor go carts are not motor vehicles for the same reason;
- earth scrapers might well be used on a road and are therefore

motor vehicles.

Mechanically Propelled Vehicle

This refers to any vehicle with mechanical transmission of power from the engine to the wheels no matter how the engine is driven – whether by petrol, oil, diesel, electricity or steam. Examples are milk floats, electrically assisted pedal cycles, electrically powered vehicles such as the Sinclair C5 and steam rollers.

Road

A "road" is any highway, and any other road to which the public has access, including a bridge.

In a decided case it was held that a road at Heathrow Airport, which was subject to various restrictions and had signs stating "No Entry Except for Access", still remained a road.

Public Place

This means a place to which the public has access. In decided cases, it has been held that the following are public places:
- a public house car park during licensing hours;
- the land leading from the berth of a cross channel ferry through the immigration and docking terminal;
- a school playground after school hours.

Accident

There is no legal definition of "accident" but the test used by the courts is whether the ordinary person, in the circumstances of the case, would conclude that there had been an accident.

Classes of Vehicle

Vehicles are divided into four classes:
Class 1: This includes most vehicles with an engine or cylinder capacity not less than 50 c.c.
Class 2: Motor vehicles and trailers authorised to carry abnormal indivisible loads; certain military vehicles and motor vehicles and trailers capable of attaining 25 m.p.h. when on the level, unladen, and not drawing a trailer.

Class 3: Motor vehicles controlled by a pedestrian, for example a lawn mower.
Class 4: All other vehicles except invalid carriages and motor cycles with an engine or cylinder capacity less than 50 c.c.

Causing and Permitting

Certain offences, such as driving otherwise than in accordance with a driving licence (see page 39) and using without insurance (page 37), may be committed not only by the driver or user, but also by a person (or a company) who causes or permits the offence.

"Causing" means giving authority to do the prohibited act. It implies a degree of control and direction, for example, an employer ordering an employee to drive without a licence.

"Permitting" is a broader term which refers to giving express or implied permission, for example, where a person lends his car to another and that other is uninsured.

Printout

There are two separate types of printout. "Printout" in motoring law means either:
- the printout produced by a breath analysis machine, which shows the proportion of alcohol in a person's breath (see page 103); or
- a printout showing a person's driving record and details of any endorsements or disqualification. This is sometimes known as a "Swansea printout" or a "DVLA printout".

DVLA

The Driver and Vehicle Licensing Authority, based in Swansea, previously known as the DVLC, Driver and Vehicle Licensing Centre.

VDRS

This stands for Vehicle Defect Rectification Scheme, under which the driver of a defective vehicle agrees to have it repaired within a certain time. If the person keeps to the agreement, the police will not issue a summons. 270,600 VDRS forms were issued in 1993; see page 66.

ATS

This stands for automatic traffic signals and means traffic lights.

Warning Formula

Also known as a notice of intended prosecution, this is the warning that must be given to persons suspected of committing certain offences. A person may not be convicted of any of these offences unless:
- he or she was warned at the time the offence was committed of the possibility of prosecution for the offence; or
- a summons was served on the person within 14 days of the offence; or
- notice of intended prosecution, specifying the nature of the alleged offence, and the time and place it is said to have been committed, is served. The notice must be served on the registered keeper of the motor vehicle if the incident involved a motor vehicle; or on the rider if it involved a cycle.

The offences to which the provision applies are:
- dangerous driving;
- driving without due care and inconsiderate driving;
- dangerous cycling;
- careless and inconsiderate cycling;
- failing to comply with a traffic direction;
- failing to comply with a traffic sign;
- leaving a vehicle in a dangerous position;
- failing to comply with a speed limit.

The requirement does not apply where there has been an accident.

Terminology Used in Court Proceedings

Summons

A summons is an official document issued by the magistrates' court setting out the offence alleged, together with brief details of the time and place where it occurred. The summons must also contain the name and address of the court, and the name or title of the person who asked for the summons to be issued, usually the Chief Superintendent of Police. The person to whom the summons is addressed is "summonsed" to appear before the court on the date and at the time specified, to answer the allegation. A summons will be sent to the last known address of the alleged offender.

A summons issued for an offence carrying not more than three months' imprisonment will also contain a statement of facts. If the person summonsed decides to plead guilty by post (see page 31), this statement will be the only information given to the court about the incident, apart from what person summonsed says about it.

Charge

If a person has been arrested, he will be "charged" rather than summonsed. This means that the details of the alleged offence will be read to him in the police station and a copy of the document setting out these matters and the date the person must attend court (the charge sheet) will be given to him.

Warrant

A warrant is a court order for the arrest of the person named in it. A warrant may be issued if:
- the summons was served a reasonable time before the hearing and the person to whom it was addressed has not responded; and
- the facts of the alleged offence have been substantiated on oath; and;
- either (a) the person is a juvenile; or (b) the offence is punishable with imprisonment; or
- the person has been convicted in his or her absence and the court proposes to disqualify.

A warrant will be issued if a person who is charged (as opposed to summonsed) does not attend court when required to do so.

Adjournment notice

An adjournment notice is a notice issued by the court telling the defendant that the case will be heard at a different date and time from those shown on the summons or previous adjournment notice.

Offence

An offence is an act or omission which is against the law.

Arrestable Offence

An arrestable offence is one in respect of which the law specifically grants to the police a power of arrest without warrant. Arrestable offences are generally those for which the maximum punishment is five years' imprisonment or more.

Serious Arrestable Offence

Some arrestable offences, such as murder or rape, are always "serious arrestable offences". Other arrestable offences will be serious if their commission leads to, for example, death, serious injury, substantial financial gain or serious financial loss. An example is causing death by dangerous driving. The consequences of an arrestable offence being deemed a serious arrestable offence include the power of the police to deny the person access to legal advice and to have someone informed that the person has been arrested, and to extend the maximum permitted period of detention before charge beyond 24 hours.

Offence of Strict Liability

This is an offence for which the offender is liable, no matter what his or her state of mind. The prosecution need only prove that the offence was committed. For example, it is an offence to use a vehicle without insurance even if the user thought he or she was insured.

Summary Offence

This is an offence which may be tried in the magistrates' court only.

Either Way Offence

Either way offences are more serious matters which may be tried either in the magistrates' court or in the Crown Court.

Indictable Offence

Indictable offences may be tried in the Crown Court only, and are the most serious matters.

Fixed Penalty Notice

A notice giving a defendant the opportunity of discharging any liability to conviction for an offence to which the fixed penalty notice relates, avoiding the possibility of being summonsed for an offence by allowing the defendant to pay a fixed penalty.

Verdict

The decision of a court as to whether a defendant is guilty or not guilty.

Evidence

Evidence is what the witnesses (including the police) say they saw or heard; certain documents, for example, a DVLC printout or a photograph produced by a Gatsometer (see page 55); and information produced by certain machines and computers, such as a printout from a Lion Intoximeter (see page 116).

Corroboration

Evidence which confirms or supports other evidence, for example, the production of speed checking equipment together with the evidence of a police officer of having seen a driver exceed the speed limit.

Trial

A hearing by the court of evidence where the defendant pleads not guilty.

Acquittal

A finding by the court that the defendant is not guilty. This is usually expressed in the magistrates' court as "the case is dismissed".

Conviction

A finding by the court that a person is guilty of an offence. This is usually expressed in the magistrates' courts as "we find the case proved".

Proof

This refers to either:
- a finding that a person is guilty (see above); or
- the trial itself, particularly if the defendant is absent, where the trial is known as a "proof in absence".

Plea

A plea is either:
- an assertion in court by the defendant that he is either guilty or not guilty; or
- a shorthand method of referring to a guilty plea.

Defendant

A person accused of an offence.

Statement

A statement is evidence which is put into writing. The prosecution may serve on a defendant what is known as a "section 9 statement" or "proof by written statement". The effect of such a notice is that the witness who made the statement will not be called to give oral evidence at court, unless the person on whom the notice is served objects (within seven days) to the statement being read. The prosecution will normally serve only fairly uncontentious statements in this manner, but if you receive one, you should carefully check to see whether you require the attendance of the witness. In a case of driving with excess alcohol, the prosecution will serve a statement from the scientist who analysed the blood. If the statement says that the reading was above 80 mg of alcohol per 100 ml of blood and you dispute this, you should not accept the statement.

Examination in Chief

Examination in chief is questioning in court by the party (the prosecution or defence) calling the witness. Only open and non-leading questions may be asked in examination in chief. A leading question is a question which suggests the answer.

Cross-Examination

Cross-examination is questioning by the party (either the prosecution or the defence) who did not call the witness. Leading questions may be asked in cross-examination, and indeed should be asked to the extent that you must put in the form of a question any part of the witness's evidence with which you disagree. For example, in a speeding case, if a police officer states in evidence that you were driving at 80 m.p.h. but you think you were driving at 70 m.p.h., you should say to the officer, "You are wrong when you say I was driving at 80 m.p.h. I put it to you that I was driving at 70 m.p.h".

Re-examination

Questioning by the party calling a witness to clarify points raised in cross-examination.

Statutory Declaration

Where it is said that a summons was served, but the person to whom is was addressed did not receive it, the person may later attend court and state on oath that he or she did not know of the proceedings or the summons. This is most usually done when a case is proved in absence, and the person is sent a notice of the penalty or a notice requiring the person to attend court because the court is considering disqualification, but the person had not received any previous correspondence from the court. A statutory declaration renders the proceedings void, but the summons may be re-issued.

Terminology Used in Sentencing

Totter

A person who has acquired 12 penalty points within three years. See page 127.

Written Plea of Guilty

A defendant who does not attend court but admits he is guilty may send a written plea of guilty by post. The summons explains how to do so. See also page 31.

Mitigation

A plea for leniency, arguments put to the court for reducing the sentence.

Standard Scale

A scale of maximum fines which may be imposed for an offence. The scales are as follows, the lower levels applying to less serious offences, and the higher levels to the more serious offences. The level applying to a particular offence is specified in the Act of Parliament creating the offence:

Level 1:	£200
Level 2:	£500
Level 3:	£1,000
Level 4:	£2,500
Level 5:	£5,000

Entry Point

The starting point for the court in deciding the punishment for an offence of average seriousness. Aggravating or mitigating factors will increase or decrease the penalty.

Costs

The successful party in court proceedings will normally be awarded costs, that is to say, a contribution towards the costs of prosecuting or defending the case. The summons will usually contain a paragraph stating that the prosecution will apply for costs. This is usually in the sum of £25 or £30, but only on a guilty plea. If you are convicted after a trial, the court may make such order as it considers to be "just and reasonable".

If you are acquitted you may apply for a "defendant's costs order" which is intended to compensate a successful defendant for any expenses properly incurred in the proceedings. It does not cover loss of earnings.

Compensation

The court may order a defendant to pay compensation for any personal injury, loss or damage which results from the commission of

the offence. In respect of road traffic offences, compensation may only be awarded:
- where the damage results from an offence under the Theft Act 1968, such as taking a conveyance or theft of a motor vehicle;
- in respect of any injury, loss or damage resulting from uninsured use of a vehicle.

Forfeiture

The court may order any property, which was in the possession of an offender and which was used in the commission of the offence, to be forfeited. This applies to a motor vehicle used in the offences of driving or attempting to drive with excess alcohol; failing to provide a specimen; failing to stop after an accident; or failing to report an accident.

The power may be exercised only in respect of road traffic offences which carry the penalty of imprisonment. If the court is considering using the power, it should grant an adjournment to allow the defendant to obtain legal advice if required.

Disqualification

See page 126.

The Magistrates' Court and its Personnel

The Magistrates

Otherwise known as Justices of the Peace or JPs, the magistrates hear the evidence and decide on the verdict and sentence. There must be a minimum of two magistrates sitting together, although it is usual to have three. Magistrates are not legally qualified and take advice from their clerk. Some courts employ a stipendiary magistrate, who is a professional lawyer and may sit alone.

Clerk

Sometimes known as a legal adviser, he or she advises the magistrates on points of law, but takes no part in the decision-making process.

Introduction

Prosecutor

A lawyer representing the Crown Prosecution Service (CPS) who presents the case for the prosecution.

Defence Solicitor or Barrister

A lawyer instructed by the defendant to defend the case or address the court in mitigation.

Duty Solicitor

Local solicitors organise a rota so that one of them is in court every day to advise and represent defendants who do not have their own solicitor. A duty solicitor will not usually represent a person charged or summonsed for a non-imprisonable offence and cannot represent a defendant at a trial.

Usher

The usher is the only person in a magistrates' court who wears a gown. He or she will register the attendance of defendants and witnesses and organise the order in which cases are to be called. You should report to the usher on your arrival in court. Unlike in the cinema, a female usher is not called an usherette.

An Outline of Magistrates' Court Procedure

It has already been noted that a case is usually begun by summons A summons is issued by the magistrates' court, and will look something like this:

ANYTOWN MAGISTRATES' COURT

SUMMONS

Date of information: 13 March 1996
Case number: 1234567
Date of summons: 21 March 1996

To: John Smith, 17 Acacia Road, Anytown, Westshire

INFORMATION HAS BEEN LAID that on 7 March 1996 at 6.30 a.m. you drove a mechanically propelled vehicle, viz a Ford Escort index number G631 VJD on a road, namely Canal Street junction with High Road, Anytown, Westshire, without due care and attention. Contrary to Section 3, Road Traffic Act 1988.

YOU ARE THEREFORE SUMMSONED to appear before the Anytown Magistrates' Court sitting at 123 High Road, Anytown, Westshire, on Monday 8th April 1996 at 10.00 a.m. to answer the above information.

Informant: Chief Superintendent Watkins, Anytown Police Station, Letzbee Avenue, Anytown, Westshire.

STATEMENT OF FACTS

On the date and time and at the place mentioned in the summons you were driving a Ford Escort in the Northbound carriageway of Canal Street. At the junction with High Street, you failed to give way to an Austin Metro which was proceeding in an Easterly direction. You collided with the Austin Metro causing damage and injury. The junction is clearly marked with a Give Way sign and Give Way markings across the carriageway. The offence was pointed out to you and you made no reply. You were told you would be reported for the offence and made no reply.

THIS OFFENCE IS ENDORSABLE WITH 3 – 9 PENALTY POINTS. YOU MUST BRING YOUR DRIVING LICENCE TO THE COURT ON THE DATE OF HEARING OR SEND IT TO THE COURT NOT LATER THAN THREE DAYS BEFORE THE HEARING. FAILURE TO DO SO IS AN OFFENCE PUNISHABLE WITH A FINE OF UP TO £1,000.00.

(Signed) .... (Justice of the Peace)

Communications relating to this Summons must quote the case number given above and should be addressed to:
The Clerk to the Justices, Anytown Magistrates' Court, 123 High Road, Anytown Westshire.
Telephone: (12345) 12345

NOTICE OF INTENTION TO ATTEND COURT OR NOTICE OF PLEA OF GUILTY

To: Anytown Magistrates' Court, 123 High Road, Anytown, Westshire
From: John Smith, 17 Acacia Road, Anytown, Westshire

Introduction

Case number: 1234567
Date of Hearing: 8th April 1996

NOTICE OF INTENTION TO ATTEND COURT
1. Do you intend to plead not guilty to the charge? yes/no
If so, please indicate how many witness(es) you intend to call: . . . . .
Please indicate any dates on which it will be inconvenient for you or your witness(es) to attend court . . . .
Signed . . . .
 2. I intend to plead guilty.
Signed . . . .
OR
NOTICE OF WRITTEN PLEA OF GUILTY
I have read the statement of facts and plead guilty to the charge. I wish the court to deal with the case in my absence and I bring to the attention of the court the statement in mitigation set out below.
Signed . . . .

The form then allows space for setting out a statement in mitigation (see page 31) and the offender's financial circumstances (see page 120).

The summons gives the date when the case will first be listed. The case will be completed on the first date of hearing only if you plead guilty (and then, not always; you may have to go back to court again if, for example, the court requires a pre-sentence report; or if the offence is endorsable and you do not bring your driving licence and the court does not have a printout). If you plead not guilty, the case will almost certainly be adjourned to a later date for trial.

Pleading Guilty

If you wish to plead guilty you may do so:
 – by attending court in person on the first date of hearing. You must bring your driving licence if the offence is endorsable (the summons will tell you if the offence is endorsable); or
 – if the offence does not carry more than three months imprisonment, you may plead guilty in writing sent by post. The summons explains how this is done. You must send your driving licence with your written plea of guilty if the offence is endorsable.

Pleading Guilty by Letter

If you wish to make a written plea of guilty, you should acknowledge receipt of the summons and clearly indicate on the form provided that you are pleading guilty. You should also complete a statement of your financial circumstances and enclose a letter in mitigation.

Never plead guilty for the sake of convenience. Do not say you are pleading guilty even though you are not guilty. The court will not accept your guilty plea, and the case will be adjourned for the witnesses to be called.

In composing a letter in mitigation, you should have regard to the following:
- keep it brief; the court may deal with up to 70 summonses in an afternoon and will lose interest if you write too much;
- express regret but avoid self-pity;
- explain the circumstances in which the offence was committed;
- make it clear that the offence was an oversight, committed in difficult weather or traffic conditions, or a momentary lapse of concentration, as appropriate;
- if appropriate, inform the court of the effect of penalty points on your employment;
- if appropriate, explain that the offence was out of character;
- express a determination not to offend again;
- ask for time to pay the fine.

An example of a letter in mitigation is set out below. The defendant has been summoned for driving at 100 m.p.h. on a motorway:

"Dear Sir or Madam

I acknowledge receipt of the summons for exceeding the speed limit on the M1 motorway on 29 February 1996.

I wish to enter a plea of guilty and accept full responsibility for the offence. On the day in question, I was travelling from my home in Manchester to attend a business meeting in London. I allowed adequate time for my journey, but I was delayed by roadworks in the city centre and reached the motorway half an hour later than anticipated.

I was anxious to reach my meeting on time and admit that I drove too fast. In the event, I failed to reach the meeting on time and did not win the contract I was seeking. I appreciate that this is no excuse, but the road surface was dry and the carriageway ahead was clear, and these factors prompted me to exceed the speed limit. I realise that this was a foolish and unacceptable way to behave.

I have held a full driving licence for twelve years and although my annual mileage is over 20,000, I have never previously committed any offence.

I am employed as a travelling sales executive and a disqualification from driving would prevent me from working. I am unable to use public transport because I need to carry a large number of heavy samples to show to potential customers. My wife and two young children are dependent on my income.

I would urge the court to regard this offence as an uncharacteristic lapse. I shall certainly be more careful in the future.

I enclose my driving licence and the completed statement of means form. I should me most grateful if you will allow me time to pay any fine.

Yours faithfully,

A Driver"

When a written plea of guilty has been received, the court proceeds as follows:
- the clerk informs the magistrates that the defendant pleads guilty by letter;
- the clerk or prosecuting lawyer reads to the court the statement of facts;
- the clerk reads to the court the letter in mitigation;
- the court decides upon the appropriate penalty;
- if the court is considering disqualification or imprisonment, the defendant will be sent a notice requiring his or her attendance at a later date – an adjournment notice (see page 21).

Pleading Guilty at Court

The procedure on a guilty plea for a summary offence where the defendant attends is as follows:
- the usher will call the defendant into court;
- the clerk will identify the defendant by asking his or her name, address and date of birth;

- the clerk will read the charge or summons, for example, "Mr [name], you are charged that on [date] you drove a mechanically propelled vehicle, namely a Ford Sierra ABC 123X, on a road, namely, High Street, Anytown, without due care and attention";
- the clerk will ask the defendant if he or she is guilty or not guilty;
- the defendant will reply "guilty". Nothing more must be said at this stage;
- the prosecutor will give the brief facts of the case and may apply for costs;
- the clerk will ask for the defendant's licence or the prosecution will produce a printout to establish the driver's record;
- the clerk will examine the defendant's licence and inform the magistrates of any relevant penalty points;
- the defendant or the defendant's lawyer will address the court in mitigation; and if appropriate may call evidence of special reasons for not endorsing or disqualifying (see page 128); or if the defendant is a "totter", may call evidence and address the court on mitigating circumstances for not disqualifying;
- the court will announce its decision, for example, "For this offence there will be a fine of £x; x penalty points will be endorsed on your licence and you will pay costs of £x";
- the defendant will usually ask for time to pay the fine.

Pleading Not Guilty

If you wish to plead not guilty, the case will not be heard on the first date of hearing, as the witnesses need to be called and court time set aside. You should send the court a notice informing them that you wish to plead not guilty, the number of witnesses you wish to call and any dates on which it would be inconvenient for you or your witnesses to attend court. As long as you send such a letter, you need not attend court on the first date. Alternatively, you can attend in person to plead not guilty.

The court will arrange a date of trial and send you an adjournment notice. If you fail to attend on that date the case may be proved in your absence. If this happens, you will be sent a notice of conviction and of the sentence imposed by the court.

If you fail to attend the trial for good reason, for example accident or illness, you may, within 28 days of conviction, apply to the court to have the case re-opened.

The following is the procedure on a not guilty hearing, otherwise known as a trial:
- as under the first five steps above;
- the prosecutor will give a brief opening speech about the allegation;
- the prosecutor will call the first witness and examine him or her in chief;
- the defence will cross-examine the prosecution witness;
- the prosecutor may re-examine the prosecution witness. The same procedure is followed in respect of each prosecution witness until;
- the prosecution closes its case. After this the prosecutor is not permitted to call further evidence;
- the defence may make a submission that there is no case to answer because the facts do not amount to an offence; or an essential feature of the offence is absent; or that the prosecution witnesses have been so discredited by cross-examination that there is no case to answer. Do not attempt to make a submission on your own; for this you will need to be represented by a lawyer. If there is clearly no case to answer, the clerk will assist you.
- the defendant calls witnesses in support of his case and examines them in chief;
- the prosecution cross-examines each witness;
- the defence may re-examine the witness;
- the defence closes its case, after which no further evidence may be called;
- a final address by the defence, summing up the points in favour of the defence case, which may lead the court to find that the defendant is not guilty;
- the court will announce its decision as to whether the defendant is guilty or not guilty;
- if the decision is that the defendant is not guilty, the defence may apply for a defendant's costs order;
- if the court finds that the defendant is guilty, then the procedure is as for a guilty plea, above.

Introduction

If you are charged rather than summsoned, you *must* attend court on every hearing. If you fail to attend, a warrant for your arrest will be issued.

Notes

- Witnesses should remain outside the court until they are called to give evidence. This is to avoid a witness's evidence being tainted by what other witnesses say.
- Witnesses may not leave the court after giving evidence without permission of the court. This is to prevent a witness who has given evidence from prompting witnesses who have not yet given evidence.
- Persons addressing the court should do so standing.
- If the defendant gives evidence he or she should do so first, before calling other witnesses. Other witnesses may give evidence before the defendant, but only with the leave of the court. Permission will usually be granted in the case of a professional witness such as a doctor.
- The court may draw such inferences as appear proper if the defendant does not give evidence. The court may infer, if no explanation is given, that the defendant does not have a defence to what the prosecution is alleging.
- In cross-examining witnesses, you should be firm but polite. It is not wise to suggest a witness is lying unless you have very strong grounds for believing that to be the case. It is far better to put your case by saying, for example, "I put it to you that you are wrong to say I was not indicating. I was indicating, wasn't I?"
- Magistrates should be addressed as "Sir" or "Madam" or "Your Worship(s)".

Chapter 2

Documents

Introduction

A motorist must comply with certain requirements concerning documents:
- A vehicle which is in use must be insured.
- A test ("MoT") certificate is required for vehicles which are still in use three years after they were first registered.
- Drivers may drive only as permitted by their driving licences; driving "otherwise that in accordance" with the licence is an offence. It is also an offence for a person who has been refused a licence, or had his or her licence revoked, to drive.
- Most vehicles must have a tax disc (or "road fund licence" or "excise licence").

Failing to meet any of these requirements amounts to an offence, and the offences are described in more detail in this chapter.

Producing Documents

A police officer may require a person who is driving a motor vehicle on a road to produce his or her insurance, driving licence and test certificate. The police may do this whether or not there has been an accident, and whether or not they suspect the driver of having committed an offence.

If the driver does not have the documents with him or her, the police will issue a form "HORT 1", also known as a "producer", or even a "seven day wonder". This is a small form on which the police officer records the name and address of the the driver; the place where the vehicle was stopped; details of the vehicle; the documents to be produced; and the police station at which the driver elects to produce them. The driver must then produce the documents at that police station within seven days. Once the form is issued, it is up to the motorist to prove that the documents exist by producing them.

Failure to Produce Documents

The Offence

It is an offence to fail to produce your insurance certificate, driving licence or test certificate to a police station within seven days of being required to do so.

Defence

If it was not reasonably practicable to produce the documents before the date on which the proceedings were commenced, it is a defence to produce them as soon as possible after the summons is issued. Examples of "reasonable impracticability" include illness, the birth of a child and mislaying the documents while moving house.

Penalties

The offence is subject to a fine up to Level 3 on the standard scale. It is not endorsable or subject to disqualification.

Using an Uninsured Vehicle

The Offence

It is an offence to use a vehicle on a road without insurance against third party risks. The offence is based on "using" rather than on driving, so that even a stationary and unattended vehicle must be insured if it is kept on a road. The third party risks which must be insured against are death or bodily injury to any person, and damage to property.

It is also an offence to "cause or permit" a motor vehicle to be on a road when it is uninsured. See page 19 for the meaning of "cause or permit".

If you are required to produce your insurance certificate, make sure you take the original certificate, not a photocopy. The police are wary of photocopies because they can be falsified. For the same reason, a cover note may not be accepted, although a cover note is included in the term "policy of insurance" provided it is in the proper form and bears a certificate that it satisfies the requirements of the relevant law.

Defence

The law allows a special defence for people who, in the course of employment, use vehicles not belonging to them or hired or loaned to them. An employee who uses an uninsured vehicle belonging to his or her employer is not guilty provided he or she did not believe, or have reason to believe, that the vehicle was uninsured.

Penalties

The courts take a serious view of using a motor vehicle without insurance, particularly if it was deliberate; if the vehicle has been used as a minicab; if no insurance has ever been held; or if the driver has previous convictions for using a vehicle without insurance.

On the other hand, the court will take a more lenient view where there has been a genuine mistake or accidental oversight; where an insurance policy has recently expired; or where responsibility for providing insurance rested on another.

The maximum fine is up to Level 5 on the standard scale. The court is obliged to endorse the driver's licence with between six and eight penalty points. It also has a discretion to disqualify the driver, and may decide to do so in a serious case. See page 125 for penalty points and page 126 for disqualification.

Using a Motor Vehicle Without a Test Certificate

A test certificate is required if a motor vehicle is still in use three years or more after it was first registered. Such certificates must be renewed every year.

The Offence

It is an offence to use or to "cause or permit the use" (see page 19 for the meaning of "cause or permit") on a road of a vehicle without a test certificate where one is required.

Defences

Imported vehicles which are normally kept abroad do not require a test certificate unless they are kept in this country for twelve months or more.

If the driver can prove that he or she was on the way to or from a test, this is a defence to a charge of not having a test certificate, but only if arrangements for the test had actually been made before the driver set out. If you have forgotten to renew your test certificate in time, it is essential to make an appointment before driving to the test centre.

As with insurance, it is for the user of the vehicle to prove that there was a test certificate. This may be difficult if the person required to produce the certificate has since sold the vehicle and passed the certificate on to the buyer. If this happens, it may be necessary to ask the test centre for a duplicate certificate.

Penalties

The maximum fine is up to Level 3 on the standard scale, but Level 4 for vehicles adapted to carry more than eight passengers. The offence is not subject to endorsement or disqualification.

Driving Otherwise than in Accordance with a Driving Licence

The Offence

This offence is awkwardly phrased, but essentially means that a driver must hold a driving licence and comply with any conditions or restrictions in the licence. The offence can be committed in a number of ways. Thus, it is an offence to drive a motor vehicle on a road if:
— the driver is under the age of seventeen;
— the vehicle is of a class not covered by the licence;
— the driver is in breach of the provisions of a provisional licence (the vehicle does not carry L plates or the driver is unsupervised);
— the driver does not have a licence at all.

Even if more than one of these provisions is breached, only one offence, the offence of driving "otherwise than in accordance" with the licence, is committed.

A driver who supervises a learner driver must:
— be at least twenty-one years of age and must have held a licence for at least three years; the licence must be to drive a vehicle of the same class as that being driven by the learner; or

— where the provisional licence is limited, the supervisor must hold a full licence authorising him or her to drive motor vehicles of a class falling within the same category as the vehicle being driven by the holder of the provisional licence.

It is also an offence to "cause or permit" (see page 19) another person to drive on a road a motor vehicle otherwise than in accordance with a licence authorising that other person to be driving the motor vehicle of that class.

Employers should be particularly careful to inspect employees' licences before allowing them to drive as part of their employment.

Defences

Holders of non-British licences may drive in Great Britain for up to twelve months after entering the country without having a British licence.

Holders of certain foreign licences may exchange their licences for British licences within twelve months of becoming resident in Great Britain. This applies to citizens of the European Union, as well as to citizens of certain other countries including Australia, Cyprus, Gibraltar, Hong Kong and New Zealand (the list changes from time to time).

Penalties

The maximum fine is up to Level 3 on the standard scale.

Endorsement with between three and six penalty points is inevitable, except where the driver could have been granted a licence, for example, where he or she omitted to renew an existing licence.

The court has a discretion to disqualify a person for driving otherwise than in accordance with his or her licence.

Driving After Refusal or Revocation of Licence

A driving licence may be refused or revoked if the applicant or holder suffers from certain medical conditions which are likely to cause driving to be a source of danger to the public. Examples of such conditions are giddiness or fainting, or inability to read in good daylight (with the aid of spectacles or contact lenses if worn) a registration mark fixed to a vehicle, containing letters 79.4

millimetres high, at a distance of 20.5 metres. An application for a driving licence must include a declaration stating whether the applicant is suffering or has suffered from such conditions.

A licence holder must declare any such condition which arises after a licence has been granted (except if the condition is likely to last for less than three months).

The Offence

It is an offence to drive a motor vehicle of any class on a road after the refusal or revocation of a licence.

A person suffering from epilepsy may be granted a driving licence if:
— the person has not suffered an epileptic fit for two years; or
— the attacks occur only during sleep; and
— the person is not likely to be a source of danger to the public if he or she drives.

Penalties

This offence is viewed seriously because it is akin to driving while disqualified (see page 93) and because it is a potential danger to other road users. For these reasons, the offence carries a maximum penalty of six months' imprisonment and/or a fine up to the maximum (currently £5,000). The offence carries obligatory endorsement with between three and six points, and disqualification is discretionary.

Using or Keeping a Vehicle Without an Excise Licence

The Offence

It is an offence to use or keep any mechanically propelled vehicle (see page 18 for the meaning of "mechanically propelled vehicle") on a public road without an excise licence in force to cover the vehicle on the day in question. Employers should note that they may be liable for the use of their untaxed vehicles by their employees.

Defence

The offence is not committed if the user can prove:
— that an application for a further licence had been made before the previous licence expired and the new licence would have

covered the day in question; and
— the expired licence was exhibited on the vehicle; and
— the period between the end of the expired licence and the day in question was not more than fourteen days.

Penalties

The offence is subject to a maximum fine up to Level 3 on the standard scale, or a fine equivalent to five times the amount of duty chargeable on the vehicle, whichever is the greater. The court will also order the back duty to be paid. It will be calculated at one-twelfth of the annual rate of duty for each calendar month or part of a month in the relevant period. The "relevant period" runs from the date when the offender notified the Driving and Vehicle Licensing Centre of the acquisition of the vehicle, or the date on which the last licence expired, whichever is later, up to the date of the offence.

The offence is not endorsable and the offender is not liable to disqualification.

Failing to Display an Excise Licence

The Offence

It is an offence if a person uses or keeps on a public road a vehicle in respect of which vehicle excise duty is chargeable and there is not fixed to and exhibited on the vehicle a current licence for the vehicle. In effect, even if you have a tax disc, it is an offence if you do not fix it, facing outwards, to the windscreen.

Defence

The offence is one of strict liability, so that it is committed even if a licence which has been fixed falls to the floor, but in such circumstances an absolute discharge will be appropriate.

It is a defence for the driver to prove that he had no reasonable opportunity to register the vehicle and that the vehicle was being driven on a public road only for the purpose of being so registered.

Penalty

The maximum fine is up to Level 1 on the standard scale. The offence is not subject to endorsement or disqualification.

Chapter 3

Standards of Driving

Motorists sometimes use the words "careless", "inconsiderate", "dangerous", "furious" or "reckless" in relation to driving as if they were interchangeable. But the law gives a distinct meaning to each of these terms and they result in entirely separate offences.

The offence of reckless driving is no longer in force because it involved a subjective element and required the courts to make difficult decisions about the driver's state of mind at the time of the offence.

In this chapter, we shall consider the following offences: driving without due care and attention (or careless driving); driving without reasonable consideration for other road users (or inconsiderate driving); dangerous driving; causing death by dangerous driving; motor manslaughter; wanton or furious driving; and motor racing on a public way.

Driving Without Due Care and Attention

The Offence

The offence is driving a mechanically propelled vehicle on a road or other public place without due care and attention (see page 18 for the meaning of "mechanically propelled vehicle"). This means that the driver fell below the standard of driving of a reasonable prudent and competent driver in the situation in which the driver was placed. The test is by reference to objective standards; it follows that it is no defence for the driver to say that he or she is young or inexperienced or even that he or she is a learner.

Sometimes the facts will speak for themselves even if there is no evidence of actual carelessness. For example, if a moving vehicle collides with a stationary vehicle and the driver cannot explain why the accident occurred, the court will be entitled to conclude that the driver must have been driving carelessly. If, on the other hand, the driver claims that he or she ran into a patch of black ice or that a sudden downpour caused the vehicle to skid, then it would be up to the prosecution to disprove the explanation.

If the driver contends that the incident was due to a mechanical defect in the vehicle, the driver will need to obtain evidence from a reputable mechanic to support the contention. The onset of the defect must have been sudden, because if you knowingly drive a defective vehicle, you may still be guilty of careless driving. If you think you may have a defence based on a mechanical defect you should obtain legal advice.

The issue in every case of careless driving is the quality of the driving and not the consequences. For this reason, the offence covers a vast range from minor bumps and near-accidents to serious injuries and even fatal accidents. Other examples include signalling one way and turning the other; failing to observe "give way" lines; and making a U-turn on a busy road. The offence will often be accompanied by another offence such as failing to obey a red traffic light or speeding on a busy road.

A breach of the Highway Code does not necessarily result in conviction; and observance of the Code does not necessarily result in acquittal. It should be noted that the Highway Code prohibits the use of hand-held telephones or microphones while driving.

The warning formula (see page 20) must be given.

Penalties

The maximum fine is Level 4 on the standard scale. Endorsement is obligatory with three to nine penalty points. Disqualification is discretionary. See page 125 for the penalty points system, and page 126 for disqualification.

The main criterion in sentencing is the degree of carelessness. The court will view the offence as more serious where there has been excessive speed or a serious risk. The court will view the offence as less serious where there were difficult weather conditions, a minor risk, a momentary lapse of concentration and negligible damage.

Driving Without Reasonable Consideration

The Offence

Driving without reasonable consideration for other persons using a road or place is an offence.

This offence does not depend on the standard of driving. All that needs to be shown is that the driver inconvenienced another road user.

People may be inconvenienced in many ways, for example, if a driver fails to keep an adequate stopping distance; fails to observe lane discipline; makes a turn from the wrong lane; cuts in front of another vehicle at a roundabout; fails to dip headlights; and even drives too slowly. Other users of the road include drivers, cyclists, pedestrians and even passengers in one's own vehicle. In every case the prosecution must prove that someone was actually inconvenienced, not merely that they *may* have been inconvenienced.

The warning formula (see page 20) must be given.

Penalties

The penalties are the same as for driving without due care and attention.

Dangerous Driving

The Offence

Driving a mechanically propelled vehicle on a road or other public place dangerously is an offence.

This is a more serious offence than careless driving because it involves a much lower standard of driving. Its seriousness is reflected in the penalties available to the court.

The offence is committed if a person drives:
(1) in a way which falls *far* below what would be expected of a competent and careful driver; and
(2) it would be obvious to a competent and careful driver that driving in that way would be dangerous; or
(3) it would be obvious to a competent and careful driver that driving the vehicle in its current state would be dangerous.

Driving in a manner "far below what may be expected of a competent and careful driver" may be contrasted with driving "which falls below the standard of driving of a reasonable, prudent and competent driver"

– the test for careless driving.

It is difficult to give examples of dangerous driving because the court will consider each case on its own facts and will have regard to the entire incident. An extreme case would involve a prolonged course of excessive speed on a busy road with the driver ignoring red traffic lights, crossing onto the opposite carriageway, causing other vehicles to swerve or brake sharply and mounting the pavement. Whether speed alone amounts to dangerous driving will depend on its degree, length, the road and traffic conditions and the time and place.

That it must be obvious to a competent and careful driver that driving in the way alleged would be dangerous (point (2) above) – is an objective test. This means that the prosecution does not need to prove that the driver was aware that his or her driving was dangerous. However, the court may have regard not only to the circumstances of which a driver could be expected to be aware, but also to any circumstances shown to have been within the driver's knowledge. If the driver knows that the vehicle is defective, and a competent and careful driver would know that the defect would make the vehicle dangerous to drive, driving the vehicle in that state will amount to dangerous driving. This is so even if the vehicle was not obviously dangerous or obviously in a dangerous condition.

Turning to (3) above, that it would be obvious to a careful and competent driver that driving the vehicle in its current state would be dangerous, we have noted that driving with a mechanical defect may amount to careless driving. The law on dangerous driving makes specific provision for mechanical defects. A person is regarded as driving dangerously if it would be obvious to a competent and careful driver that driving the vehicle in its current state would be dangerous. For example, a person may be convicted of dangerous driving if he drives with defective brakes, defective steering or a defective or dangerously worn tyre, provided it would be obvious to a competent and careful driver that this would be dangerous. In determining the state of the vehicle, the court may take into consideration anything attached to it or carried on or in it, and the manner in which the thing is attached or carried, for example, carrying an insecure load in a manner which, to a competent and careful driver, would obviously be dangerous.

The Effect of Alcohol on Dangerous Driving

The fact that a driver was adversely affected by drink is relevant to whether he or she was driving dangerously. It must be shown that the amount of drink consumed was such as would adversely affect a driver; or, alternatively, that the driver was in fact adversely affected.

Penalties

This offence may be tried either at the magistrates' court or at the Crown Court. In a magistrates' court, the maximum sentence is six months' imprisonment and/or a fine up to the legal maximum. In the Crown Court, the maximum sentence is two years' imprisonment and/or an unlimited fine.

The offence carries obligatory disqualification for a minimum of twelve months and a compulsory retest. If there are special reasons for not disqualifying (see page 128), the licence must be endorsed with three to eleven penalty points.

The entry point (see page 26) for this offence is a community penalty. Aggravating features will include:
- whether the offence was committed while on bail;
- whether the driver attempted to avoid detection or apprehension;
- competitive driving, racing or showing off;
- disregard of warnings, for example from passengers or others in the vicinity;
- evidence of alcohol or drugs;
- excessive speed;
- the likelihood of serious risk;
- previous convictions; and
- failure to respond to previous sentences.

On the other hand, the following will go towards mitigation:
- risk which was not fully appreciated;
- the absence of alcohol or drugs;
- a single incident.

In considering sentence, the court will take into account the age and health of the offender; cooperation with the police; whether or not the offender has paid compensation voluntarily; and any expression of remorse. However, a plea of guilty will not attract a discount from the maximum sentence where the offender had no realistic option but to plead guilty.

Alternative Verdict

If the magistrates' court, or the jury in the Crown Court, does not find a charge of dangerous driving proved, but does find the defendant guilty of one of the lesser offences of careless driving or inconsiderate driving, the court can find the driver not guilty of dangerous driving, but guilty of the lesser offence. This is known as an "alternative verdict".

Causing Death by Dangerous Driving

The Offence

Causing the death of another person by driving a mechanically propelled vehicle on a road or other public place by dangerous driving is an offence. The meaning of "dangerous" is as for dangerous driving.

In view of the seriousness of the offence, it can be tried only at the Crown Court.

"Causation"

The cause of death must be connected with the driving complained of, but driving need not be the only or main cause of death.

The court may take into account anything attached to or carried on or in the vehicle, and the manner in which it is attached or carried. It follows that a driver who carries an insecure and heavy load may be convicted of causing death by dangerous driving if the load falls and kills another road user, provided either that the driver knew the load was insecure or it would be obvious to a competent and careful driver that driving the vehicle in that state would be dangerous.

For the offence to be committed, death must occur within one year and one day of the act of dangerous driving, although this aspect of the law of homicide is currently being reviewed by government.

Other Persons

"Another person" means another driver, a passenger in another vehicle or a pedestrian. A Scottish Court has held that the term "another person" includes an unborn child.

Standards of Driving

Alternative verdicts

On a charge of causing death by dangerous driving the jury may, if it does not find that charge proved, instead convict the driver of any of the following offences it finds proved:
- dangerous driving;
- wanton and and furious driving;
- careless or inconsiderate driving.

Penalties

The maximum penalty is ten years' imprisonment. Disqualification for a minimum of two years is obligatory, with a compulsory extended test (see page 126). If there are special reasons for not disqualifying (see page 128), the licence must be endorsed with three to eleven penalty points.

The main concern of the court in sentencing is the criminality of the driver; death itself is a factor contributing to the length of the sentence. The Court of Appeal has emphasised that it will not be persuaded by public or press campaigns to increase sentences; nor will it be influenced by personal factors of mitigation such as remorse.

The extremely serious nature of this offence and the likely sentence make it essential for anyone charged with causing death by dangerous driving to obtain legal advice at an early stage.

Motor Manslaughter

The Offence

There is no separate offence of "motor manslaughter" but the general law of manslaughter may apply where death is caused by the driver of a motor vehicle. "Manslaughter" means the unlawful killing of another person but, unlike murder, does not require an intent to kill or to cause serious bodily injury.

The offence of manslaughter, unlike causing death by dangerous driving, is not restricted to driving. However, the offence will be charged only where the circumstances are very grave, such as where a driver exhibits hostile intent. An example is where death results from a driver deliberately driving in the direction of a pedestrian, although such a driver might also be charged with murder.

Penalties

A charge of manslaughter may be tried only at the Crown Court. The maximum sentence is life imprisonment and/or an unlimited fine. Disqualification is obligatory, as is a compulsory retest. If there are special reasons for not disqualifying (see page 126), then the licence is endorsed with three to eleven points. The Court of Appeal has held that the sentence for motor manslaughter should not be limited to that for causing death by dangerous driving.

The alternative verdict of causing death by dangerous driving is not available to a jury which acquits the defendant of manslaughter.

Wanton or Furious Driving

The Offence

This offence applies to mechanically propelled vehicles, cycles and other carriages driven anywhere *other than* on a road or in a public place. It is therefore possible for a person who drives a horse-drawn carriage on a private field to be charged with this offence.

The prosecution must prove that the defendant was in charge of a carriage or vehicle and by wanton driving or racing, or by furious driving or racing, or by wilful misconduct or by wilful neglect, did or caused to be done any bodily harm to any person.

Penalties

The charge may be tried only at the Crown Court. The maximum penalty is two years' imprisonment. The offence is not endorsable and is not subject to disqualification.

Motor Racing

The Offence

The offence involves the commission of or taking part in a race or a trial between motor vehicles on public ways. At least two vehicles must be involved.

Defences

Competitions or trials (but not races or trials of speed) may be held on a public way if they are authorised by the Secretary of State and conducted in accordance with any conditions imposed.

Penalties

The penalties are as follows:
- a fine up to Level 4 on the standard scale;
- obligatory disqualification for a minimum of twelve months;
- if there are special reasons for not disqualifying (see page 128), obligatory endorsement with three to eleven points.

Chapter 4

Speeding

With the exception of parking offences, speeding is the offence most likely to be committed by ordinary motorists. There are several different types of speeding offence, and even this seemingly simple offence has complications in relation to evidence. In this chapter we shall examine the ways in which the offence may be committed and the evidence that is required in relation to each category of speeding offence.

Types of Speeding Offence

There are five categories of offence:
- exceeding the limit on a restricted road;
- exceeding a temporary limit or restriction on roads other than motorways;
- exceeding the limit on any road applicable to a particular class of vehicle;
- exceeding the limit imposed by local authorities;
- exceeding the limit on a motorway.

Exceeding the Limit on a Restricted Road

The Offence

Driving a motor vehicle on a restricted road at a speed exceeding 30 miles an hour is an offence.

Meaning of Restricted Road

A road is a restricted road if it has street lamps which are not more than 200 yards apart. This requirement is not construed strictly by the courts, and a road with some lamps more than 200 yards apart will still be a restricted road. If the requirement is breached in more than a minimal way, then the driver may have a defence. In such cases it is advisable either to take one's own measurements or, better still, to obtain street plans from the traffic authority.

The traffic authority for a road may direct:
- that a restricted road shall cease to be a restricted road for the purpose of the 30 mile per hour limit; or
- that a road which is not a restricted road shall be deemed a restricted road for that purpose.

Where there is no street lighting but there is a speed limit, the limit must be indicated by traffic signs. If there is no street lighting and no traffic signs, a driver cannot be convicted of exceeding the speed limit on a restricted road.

Where there are no traffic signs on a road with street lighting, the fact that there are no traffic signs to indicate that the road is not restricted is evidence that the road is a restricted road.

It is no defence for a driver to say that he or she did not see the signs or did not know the road was restricted to 30 miles an hour. However, it is perfectly possible for there to be lighting which is not street lighting. In one case it was held that the lighting was not street lighting but lighting for a nearby promenade. The driver was therefore not convicted of exceeding the speed limit on a restricted road.

Exceeding a Temporary Limit or Restriction on Roads other than Motorways

There is a difference between a temporary speed limit and a temporary speed restriction and we shall deal with each of them in turn.

Speed Limits

Temporary maximum and minimum speed limits may be made in the interests of safety or to facilitate the movement of traffic.

The current "temporary" speed limits have been "temporary" since 1977. They are 70 m.p.h. on an unrestricted dual carriageway and 60 m.p.h. on an unrestricted single carriageway.

There is no need for there to be signs to this effect, but a traffic authority must erect signs where a maximum limit applies to a particular stretch of road.

Although the power to establish minimum speed limits exists, at the time of writing no minimum speed limits have been set. If minimum speed limits are established, signs must be displayed indicating that speed.

Speed Restrictions

The highway authority may impose restrictions for the purposes of roadworks, cleaning, administration or for any purpose to prevent danger to the public.

Exceeding the Limit Applicable to a Particular Class of Vehicle

Some vehicles are subject to speed limits whether or not they are on a a restricted road. Ordinary cars with an unladen weight less than 3.05 tonnes, motor cycles and caravans are not subject to this restriction unless they are adapted to carry more than eight passengers or are drawing a trailer. Vehicles adapted to carry more than eight passengers excluding the driver, are subject to:
- a 70 m.p.h. limit on motorways;
- a 60 m.p.h. limit on dual carriageways; and
- a 50 m.p.h. limit on other roads.

Passenger vehicles exceeding 12 metres in length are subject to:
- a 60 m.p.h. limit on motorways and dual carriageways;
- a 50 m.p.h. limit on other roads while drawing a trailer; and
- a 40 m.p.h. limit on motorways; and
- a 20 m.p.h. limit elsewhere if more than one trailer is being drawn.

Invalid carriages are not permitted on motorways and are subject to a 20 m.p.h. limit on all other roads.

Other restrictions apply to goods vehicles, motor tractors, works trucks, industrial tractors and agricultural motor vehicles, but these are outside the scope of this book.

Exceeding the Limit Imposed by a Local Authority

A local authority may vary speed limits within its area. The authority may impose speed restrictions either temporarily or permanently or during particular times of the day.

Exceeding the Limit on a Motorway

The overall speed limit on motorways is 70 m.p.h. A sign need only be displayed where a different overall limit is in force.

Exemption for the Fire Brigade, Police and Ambulance Service

None of the speed limits apply to any vehicle when it is being used for fire brigade, ambulance or police purposes, if observing the limit would be likely to hinder the use of the vehicle for that purpose.

Evidence

A driver may not be convicted of exceeding the speed limit solely on the evidence of one witness that, in the opinion of that witness, the driver was exceeding the speed limit.

This does not apply to exceeding a speed *restriction* because a restriction is not a limit. Nor does it apply to exceeding the overall limit on a motorway.

In all other cases, the law requires corroboration (for the meaning of "corroboration" see page 23). Corroboration may be in the form of:
- another witness. The evidence must relate to the same piece of driving;
- the speedometer of a police vehicle, provided that it is properly calibrated;
- skid marks or expert evidence in relation to impact damage or accident reconstruction. In such cases the prosecution should inform the defence in advance of the evidence on which they seek to rely;
- speed checking equipment such as a radar gun. This is a device which transmits a radar beam at a vehicle as it passes the device;
- Vascar (Visual Average Speed Computer and Recorder). This is a device which records the average speed of a vehicle by reference to its speed over a known distance;
- Gatsometer. This is an automatic camera affixed to the roadside to detect speeding (and traffic light) offences. It is named after its inventor, Maurice Gatsonides, a former racing driver.

The warning formula (see page 20) must be given.

Speeding

Penalties

The penalties for exceeding a speed limit are :
- a fine up to Level 3 on the standard scale, but up to Level 4 where the offence is committed on a motorway;
- endorsement with three to six penalty points except where the offence is dealt with by way of a fixed penalty (see page 121) in which case three points are imposed; and
- discretionary disqualification. The court will consider disqualification if the speed was 30 m.p.h. or more over the limit. You should expect disqualification for seven days if your speed is 30 to 34 m.p.h. over the limit; 14 days if 35 to 39 m.p.h. over the limit; and a minimum of 21 days if your speed is 40 m.p.h. or more over the limit.

Chapter 5

Motorways

Introduction

Certain regulations apply to motorways, which are known in the regulations as "special roads". The definition of a special road is tautological in that a special road is one which may be used only by vehicles of class 1 and class 2 (see page 18), and one of the offences in connection with motorways is driving a motor vehicle of the wrong class.

A number of offences may be committed on motorways only, and these include:
- driving otherwise than on a carriageway;
- driving in the wrong direction;
- making a U-turn;
- stopping on the carriageway;
- using the hard shoulder;
- reversing on the motorway;
- using the central reservation or verge;
- use of the motorway by a learner driver;
- use of the right hand lane;
- offences concerning animals;
- driving a vehicle of the wrong class; and
- use of a motorway by a pedestrian.

Driving Otherwise than on a Carriageway

It is an offence to drive on any part of a motorway which is not a carriageway. "Carriageway" means that part of the motorway which is provided for the regular passage of traffic along the motorway. The central reservation and the hard shoulder are not parts of the carriageway and it is an offence to drive on them.

Driving in the Wrong Direction

It is an offence to drive or move a vehicle onto the carriageway at a place where there is a "no entry" sign; or to contravene a traffic sign indicating "no left turn" or "no right turn".

It is an offence to drive in a direction so that the central reservation is not on the right hand side or off-side of the vehicle. That is to say, motorists must drive to the left of the central reservation.

An exception is where a contra-flow system is in operation. Contra-flow means a part of the carriageway where:
- traffic is authorised to proceed in the opposite direction to the usual direction on that part; or
- a specified class of traffic is authorised to proceed in the opposite direction to other traffic on that carriageway.

U-Turns

It is an offence to drive or move a vehicle so as to cause it to turn and proceed in or face the opposite direction. In other words, U-turns are forbidden.

Stopping

It is an offence to stop or to remain at rest on a carriageway except in the following circumstances:
- by reason of a breakdown or mechanical defect, or lack of fuel or water required for the vehicle; or
- by reason of accident, illness or any other emergency; or
- to permit the driver or a passenger to recover or remove any object which has fallen onto a motorway; or
- to permit the driver or a passenger to help any other person in any of the circumstances specified above.

In such a case, the vehicle should, as far as is reasonably practicable, be driven or moved off the carriageway, and may stop on the hard shoulder which is contiguous to the carriageway. But it must not be left there for longer than is necessary for the particular purpose specified above.

A vehicle on the hard shoulder should, as far as reasonably practicable, be in such a position that no part of it or its load causes any obstruction or danger to vehicles using the carriageway.

A vehicle may stop or remain at rest on a carriageway when it is prevented from proceeding along the carriageway by the presence of any other vehicle, or any person or object, for example, in a traffic jam or where a vehicle ahead has shed its load.

Reversing

It is an offence to drive or move backwards on a motorway, except in so far as it is necessary to back the vehicle to enable it to proceed forwards or to be connected to any other vehicle, for example, following an accident or to connect to a recovery vehicle.

Using the Central Reservation or Verge

It is an offence to drive or move or stop or remain at rest on a central reservation or verge.

Learner Drivers

It is an offence to drive a vehicle on a motorway if the driver holds only a provisional licence, unless the driver has passed a test authorising him to drive that vehicle.

The Right Hand Lane

It is an offence for certain vehicles to use the right hand lane (or off-side lane) of a carriageway which has three or more traffic lanes where all the lanes are open for use by traffic proceeding in the same direction.

The vehicles which may not use the right hand are:
- goods vehicles with a maximum laden weight exceeding 7.5 tonnes;
- motor vehicles constructed solely for the carriage of passengers which exceed 12 metres in length, such as certain buses and coaches, including public service vehicles, school buses and works buses;
- motor vehicles drawing trailers; and
- motor tractors, light locomotives or heavy locomotives.

A vehicle of this kind may, however, use the off-side lane if necessary to enable it to pass another vehicle which is carrying or drawing an exceptionally wide load. But a vehicle may not change lane when it would not be reasonably practicable to do so without involving danger of injury to any person or inconvenience to other traffic.

Animals

A person in charge of an animal carried by a vehicle using a motorway must ensure that the animal does not leave the vehicle.

If it escapes, or if it is necessary for it to be removed from the vehicle, or if it is permitted to leave the vehicle, for example by a police officer, the animal must remain on the hard shoulder and it must be held on a lead or otherwise kept under proper control.

Excluded Traffic

Vehicles of classes 3 and 4 (see page 19) may not be used on a motorway except for such purposes as maintenance, repair and cleaning.

Pedestrians

It is an offence to walk on a motorway.

General Defences

It is a defence to any of the matters discussed in this chapter if the act in question was done:
- in accordance with any direction or permission given by a police constable in uniform or in accordance with a traffic sign;
- in accordance with any permission given by a constable for the purpose of investigating an accident which has occurred on or near the motorway;
- to avoid or prevent an accident or to obtain or give help following an accident or emergency, provided that the act is done so as to cause as little danger or inconvenience as possible to other traffic on the motorway;
- where the act is done by a constable, or a member of the fire brigade or ambulance service, in the exercise of the person's duty;
- to carry out maintenance, repair and cleaning.

Penalties

All motorway offences are subject to a fine up to Level 4 on the standard scale. They are all endorsable and subject to discretionary disqualification, except for stopping on the hard shoulder and walking on the motorway. The court will consider disqualification for driving in the wrong direction and making a U-turn, as well as for speeding in excess of 30 m.p.h. over the limit.

Chapter 6

Construction and Use

Introduction

The regulations governing the construction and use of vehicles are very wide in scope. They concern, for example, the emission or consumption of smoke, fumes or vapour; noise; the unladen weight of heavy motor cars; the towing or drawing of vehicles; the number and nature of brakes; lighting equipment and reflectors; silencers; steering gear; and tyres. Many of the requirements concern how vehicles are built in the first place, and so apply only to vehicle manufacturers. Others regulate the condition of motor vehicles while in use, and create a number of offences which can be committed by drivers. This chapter deals only with those offences which are endorsable.

The endorsable offences are as follows:
- the general offence of using a vehicle in a dangerous condition;
- offences in connection with brakes;
- offences in connection with steering gear; and
- offences in connection with tyres.

Using a Vehicle in Dangerous Condition

It is an offence to use, or to cause or permit another person to use (see page 19 for the meaning of "cause or permit"), a motor vehicle or trailer in such a way that it involves danger of injury to any person. Danger may arise from:
- the condition of the motor vehicle or trailer or of its accessories or equipment; or
- the purpose for which it is used; or
- the number of passengers carried in it or the manner in which they are carried; or
- the weight, position or distribution of its load or the manner in

which the load is secured.

Condition of the Vehicle

The most obvious examples of vehicles in a dangerous condition include those with defective brakes, tyres or steering gear, although these defects may be the subject of separate offences; see below. A vehicle may also be in a dangerous condition if, for instance, the exhaust system is wrongly positioned so as to risk burning pedestrians; or if there has been accident damage to the body of the vehicle, leaving sharp or protruding edges which could cause injury.

It is no defence to say that the condition of the vehicle is a result of the way it was constructed. You may still be committing an offence if the construction of the vehicle presents a danger of injury to any person. It is therefore arguable that the "bull bars" on some four-wheel drive vehicles may contravene these regulations. In a decided case it was held that the unguarded spikes of a mechanical digger can amount to a contravention of this regulation and therefore an offence.

The Purpose for Which a Vehicle is Used

"Unsuitable use" includes carrying an unsuitable load, for example carrying a heavy load or a long ladder on the roof of an ordinary car. In a decided case, the driver of a lorry loaded with two fork-lift trucks attempted to pass under a foot bridge. It was held that this was an unsuitable use having regard to the route taken. Another example of "unsuitable use" is where a scrambling motor cycle is used on a road. Such vehicles are fitted with special "knobbly" tyres which are unsuitable for use on the road because the rubber does not properly adhere to the road surface.

Passengers

The number of passengers carried, or the way they are carried, will amount to a danger where, for example, a saloon car designed for four passengers is carrying eight passengers. If the driver's rear view is obscured by passengers, this may amount not only to driving a vehicle in a dangerous condition, but also to careless driving (see page 43).

Loads

A vehicle will be in a dangerous condition, if, for example, it is carrying a load which is too heavy, badly positioned or not distributed evenly.

In all cases of driving a vehicle in a dangerous condition, the prosecution must prove that using the vehicle posed a danger of injury to any person.

Tyres

A motor vehicle or trailer must not be used on a road if:
- a tyre is unsuitable having regard to the use to which the motor vehicle or trailer is being put, or to the types of tyres fitted to its other wheels;
- a tyre is inflated in a way which makes it unfit for the use to which the motor vehicle or trailer is being put, for example, tyres should be inflated to a higher degree of pressure when the vehicle or trailer is carrying a heavy load. If a tyre is under-inflated, the offence will be committed;
- a tyre has a cut in excess of 25 mm or 10 per cent of the section width (ie across the fabric) of the tyre, whichever is the greater, measured in any direction on the outside of the tyre and deep enough to reach the ply or cord;
- a tyre has any lump, bulge or tear caused by separation or partial failure of its structure;
- a tyre has any ply or cord exposed;
- the base of the groove which showed in the original groove tread pattern of the tyre is not clearly visible;
- either (a) the grooves of the tread pattern of the tyre do not have a depth of at least 1.6 mm throughout a continuous band measuring at least three quarters of the breadth of the tread and round the entire outer circumference of the tyre; or (b) the grooves of the original tread pattern of the tyre do not extend beyond three quarters of the breadth of the tread, or any groove which showed in the original tread pattern does not have a depth at least 1.6 mm;
- a tyre is not maintained in such condition as to be fit for the use to which the vehicle or trailer is being put, or has a defect which might in any way cause damage to the surface of the road or to

persons on or in the vehicle or to other persons using the road.
If more than one tyre is said to be defective, a separate summons will be issued for each. This will have a considerable effect on the number of penalty points endorsed on the licence if the driver pleads guilty or is found guilty.

Brakes

Every part of the braking system and the means of operating the brakes must be maintained in good and efficient working order and be properly adjusted.

Steering Gear

The steering fitted to a motor vehicle must at all times be maintained in good and efficient working order and be properly adjusted.

Strict Liability

These offences are offences of strict liability. This means that the driver can be guilty of an offence even if not at fault and even if unaware that there was a defect. The only defence is to show that it is not correct to say that the vehicle was in a dangerous condition. Whether or not this can be argued will depend on the facts of the particular case, and may mean getting evidence from a mechanic or motor engineer about the state of the vehicle. But in a "causing or permitting" case the prosecution must prove that the person said to have caused or permitted the offence knew of the fault. Likewise, for a company to be guilty of causing or permitting, it must be shown that someone in control of the company, or at least somebody with authority, was aware of the defect.

Penalties

The penalties for the "construction and use" offences discussed above are:
- a fine up to Level 4 on the standard scale, but up to Level 5 in respect of goods vehicles or vehicles adapted to carrying more than eight passengers;
- endorsement with three penalty points;

– discretionary disqualification.

Because the offences are offences of strict liability, the court will always have regard to the degree of responsibility of the driver.

The driver should not be disqualified or have his licence endorsed if he or she proves that there are special reasons for not doing so (see page 128); or if the driver establishes that he or she did not know, and had no reason to suspect, that an offence was being committed. This argument may well be open to a person who carries out proper maintenance or checks on the vehicle, or, perhaps, has had the vehicle recently serviced. It is also available to an employee who uses a company vehicle after being assured by the management that it is in proper condition.

On the other hand, employers who give express instructions to employees about what to do if defects occur may also be able to use this argument if they are summonsed for "causing or permitting" the offence and the employee in question did not follow instructions. Most road haulage companies require their employees to check tyres, steering, brakes and windscreen before taking a vehicle out on a journey; written evidence of such instructions will greatly assist an employer who is accused of causing or permitting an employee to drive a defective vehicle.

The Vehicle Defect Rectification Scheme

The vehicles defect rectification scheme was introduced to encourage drivers to repair defective vehicles. Often, particularly in the case of relatively minor defects, the police will issue a "Vehicle Defects – Notice to Driver". This is a small form on which the officer completes details of the driver, the vehicle and the defect(s). The driver can avoid being prosecuted by having the vehicle repaired by an approved garage. If the garage is satisfied that the defects have been satisfactorily repaired, it endorses the form to that effect and the driver then sends the form back to the police. In most areas this must be done within 14 days of the date the notice is issued.

Chapter 7

Accidents

Introduction

A driver is not required to stop after every accident, but must stop or report an accident which results in either personal injury (this may include nervous shock) to another person, or damage to another vehicle or trailer or to an animal or roadside property. "Animal" in this context does not include an animal in the vehicle or trailer driven by the driver in question; nor does it include wild animals such as rabbits, squirrels, hedgehogs, foxes or mice. It does include horses, cattle, asses, mules, sheep, pigs, goats and dogs (but not cats).

Failing to Stop After an Accident

This offence is committed if the driver does not stop after an accident, or if, having stopped, fails to give his or her name and address, the name and address of the owner of the vehicle (if it is owned by someone else), and its registration number, to a person having reasonable grounds to require this information. This will obviously include any person who is injured or any person whose property has been damaged; and may also include a friend or relation of a person who was injured or whose property was damaged.

The requirement to stop includes a requirement to remain at the scene of the accident for as long as is appropriate in the circumstances. The court will generally be sympathetic to persons who do not stop because it might be dangerous to do so, for example, a woman who fails to stop at night in what is considered a dangerous area.

Failing to Report an Accident

This offence is committed when a person has failed to stop after an accident and does not then report it at a police station or to a constable as soon as is reasonably practicable, and in any case within 24 hours of the accident. It is not necessary to report the accident immediately. A person who could have reported an accident sooner than he or she in fact did report it is not necessarily guilty of the offence, but the person may be convicted if there was an unreasonable delay, even if the report was made within the 24 hour period. Each case will be decided on its own facts.

If you have stopped and given your name and address, the name and address of the owner of the vehicle and its registration number, to a person having reasonable grounds for requiring these details, then you cannot be guilty of failing to report. The offence of failing to report arises only when a person has failed to stop after an accident.

Failing to Produce an Insurance Certificate Following a Personal Injury Accident

If the driver of a motor vehicle does not at the time of an accident produce a certificate of insurance to a constable or to some other person who, having reasonable grounds for so doing, has required him to produce it, the driver must report the accident and produce his or her certificate of insurance at a police station or to a constable as soon as is reasonably practicable and in any case within 24 hours of the accident.

The offence is not committed if the certificate is produced within seven days after the accident at the police station specified by the driver at the time the accident was reported (see page 15).

Defence

It is a defence for the driver to prove that he or she was not aware that an accident had occurred. However, as soon as you become aware that an accident has occurred, the duty to report arises from that time.

Penalties

The offences of failing to stop and failing to report (but not failure to produce an insurance certificate) render the offender liable to six months' imprisonment and/or a fine not exceeding Level 5 on the standard scale. Endorsement with five to ten penalty points is obligatory, and disqualification is discretionary.

Many drivers do not realise the seriousness of these offences or that they are punishable with imprisonment. The court has had power to imprison for these offences since the Road Traffic Act 1991, which came into force in July 1992.

Imprisonment may seem a harsh penalty for these offences, but the equivalent provision following a collision at sea renders the offender liable to imprisonment for five years. Imprisonment will generally be reserved for the worst cases, such as "hit and run" accidents where the driver does not help a person who is injured. At the other end of the scale are the least serious offences which involve minor bumps and "prangs" where there is no personal injury and only minor damage. In such cases the offender is likely to be given the minimum five penalty points. The penalty is also likely to be lower where the driver failed to stop but did report the accident; where the driver stayed at the scene but failed to give full particulars or left before giving full particulars; or where there was no one at the scene, but the driver failed to report within the requisite 24 hours.

Most insurance policies require the policy-holder to report any accident to the insurers. It is particularly important for holders of comprehensive policies to do so if someone else is saying that the policy holder was responsible for the accident. The reason is that if civil proceedings are brought, they will be defended by the insurance company, and not the policy holder in person.

Chapter 8

Traffic Directions and Traffic Signs

Failing to Comply with a Direction Given by a Constable

The offence

It is an offence to neglect or refuse to comply with a direction given by a constable or traffic warden to stop a vehicle, or make it proceed, or keep to a particular line of traffic. For the offence to be committed, the constable or warden must be regulating traffic or conducting a traffic survey when giving the direction. There is no duty to participate in a traffic survey, but a driver must stop the vehicle or make it proceed or keep to a particular line of traffic when required to do so.

The warning formula (see page 20) must be given.

Defence

It is a defence for the driver to prove that he or she was unaware that a direction had been given. This will be difficult to prove and is most likely to succeed where the constable did not make his or her intentions clear, or where visibility was poor.

Penalties

- A fine up to Level 3 on the standard scale;
- obligatory endorsement with three penalty points;
- discretionary disqualification.

Failing to Comply with a Traffic Sign

Unlike the offence in connection with directions (above), this offence does not involve neglect or refusal, but simply failure to comply. It is therefore no defence for a driver to say that he or she did not see the

sign. The offence is committed by failing to comply with any of the following traffic signs:
- stop;
- give way;
- stop one way working (a temporary stop sign used where one-way working is necessary owing to a temporary closure of part of the width of the carriageway);
- no entry;
- directional arrows;
- arrows indicating keep left or right;
- red lights;
- double white lines;
- keep left, dual carriageway;
- turn left at dual carriageway;
- prohibition of U-turn;
- mini roundabout;
- green arrow light signals;
- mandatory height restriction;
- yellow box junctions.

We shall now consider in more detail some of the more common offences of failing to comply with traffic signs.

Traffic Lights

It is an offence to fail to stop at a red traffic light. You must also stop when the light is amber with red. You should not proceed beyond the amber alone light unless you are so close to the line (or post or structure if the line is not clearly visible) that it would be unsafe to stop before passing the line, post or structure. Failure to comply with the amber alone signal is not an offence, but in some circumstances it may amount to careless driving.

It is also an offence to fail to comply with the four intermittent red signals displayed on motorways or at the alternately flashing red lights at level crossings, lifting bridges, airfields, fire stations and tunnels.

Even when the green light shows in your favour you must proceed with due regard to the safety of other road users.

Stop Signs

It is an offence to fail to comply with an octagonal stop sign at a road junction. You must stop your vehicle before crossing the white transverse line, but if the line is not clearly visible, you must stop before entering the major road. You should not enter the major road so as to be likely to cause danger to any other driver or to cause another driver to change speed or direction to avoid an accident.

The warning formula (see page 20) must be given.

Give Way Signs

It is an offence to fail to comply with a give way sign used in conjunction with a transverse line and a triangle painted on the road. You must not cross the line nearest the major road or enter the major road so as to be likely to cause danger to another driver or to cause another driver to change speed or direction to avoid an accident.

Defences

The offence is one of strict liability (see page 22).

White Lines

Lines or marks on the road may be "traffic signs" for these purposes if they indicate a warning, prohibition, restriction or requirement. A single white line is not a "traffic sign", but failure to comply with a single white line may in some circumstances amount to careless driving.

Where there are double white lines, one of which is continuous and the other is broken, you must keep to the left of the continuous white line if it is the nearer of the two. You must not stop on either side of a road within a double white line system even if only one white line is continuous.

It is a defence to allow a vehicle to cross or straddle the continuous white line:
- to obtain access to side roads, land or premises adjoining the road;
- to avoid an accident;
- in circumstances beyond the driver's control; or
- under the direction of a uniformed police constable or traffic

warden.

Penalties

- a maximum fine up to Level 3 on the standard scale;
- endorsement with three penalty points if the vehicle was a motor vehicle and the traffic sign was a stop sign, red traffic light or double white lines; where the driver breached a prohibition on vehicles over a certain height; and for the offence of not obtaining permission to cross a railway level crossing by the driver of an abnormal load;
- discretionary disqualification.

Chapter 9

Pedestrian Crossings

There are two types of pedestrian crossing:
- zebra (uncontrolled crossings) and
- pelican (controlled crossings).

Zebra Crossings

These are identified by:
- two lines of studs across the roadway;
- black and white stripes on the crossing itself;
- yellow globes mounted on posts or brackets on each end of the crossing which are illuminated by flashing, or, in some circumstances, constant, light;
- at one metre each side of the crossing there is a broken white "give way" line and zig zag lines indicating the extent of the controlled area.

Pelican Crossings

These are non-automatic traffic lights which are controlled by pedestrians. Pelican crossings consist of a combination of:
- traffic light signals;
- pedestrian light signals; and
- indicators for pedestrians (a push button or pressure pad).

The layout of a pelican crossing depends on whether there is a central reservation or a staggered crossing, and whether the crossing is in a one-way street.

A pelican crossing is indicated by:
- two lines of studs across the carriageway;
- a stop line on the carriageway which is parallel to the nearest row of studs, indicating the limits of the crossing; and

- two or more zig zag lines on the carriageway.

This chapter deals with the following offences:
- failing to accord precedence on a zebra crossing;
- stopping in a zebra-controlled area;
- overtaking on a zebra crossing;
- failing to accord precedence on a pelican crossing; and
- stopping in an area adjacent to a pelican crossing.

Failure to Accord Precedence on a Zebra Crossing

It is an offence to fail to accord precedence to a pedestrian who is on the carriageway within the limits of the crossing before the vehicle or any part of it is within the limits.

For these purposes, the "limits" means the black and white striped area and not the zig-zag lines denoting the limits of the controlled area. The vehicle must stop at or before the give way lines. If there is a traffic island in the middle of the road, then each side of the zebra crossing is treated separately.

If a pedestrian is pushing a pram or push chair, you must stop when the pram or push chair is on the crossing even if the pedestrian is on the pavement.

To accord precedence means that you should not interfere with the pedestrian's right of passage on the crossing.

You must drive in such a way as to enable the vehicle to stop at the crossing unless it is clear that there is no one on it. In practical terms, this means that you must reduce speed when approaching a zebra crossing.

Stopping in a Zebra-Controlled Area

It is an offence to stop in the zebra-controlled area. This includes the further side of the crossing as well as the approach to it. For these purposes, the controlled area is the area marked by the zig-zag lines, not just the crossing itself.

The offence cannot be committed by the rider of a bicycle unless there is a side car attached.

Overtaking in a Zebra-Controlled Area

It is an offence, when approaching a zebra crossing, to overtake a moving motor vehicle or any stationary vehicle including a bicycle. A "stationary vehicle" for these purposes means a vehicle which has stopped to allow pedestrians to cross.

Failure to Afford Precedence on a Pelican Crossing

It is an offence to fail to accord precedence to a pedestrian on a pelican crossing if the pedestrian is on the carriageway or central reservation (unless it is a staggered crossing where the traffic light signal shows a flashing amber light).

Stopping in an Area Adjacent to a Pelican Crossing

It is an offence to stop in areas adjacent to pelican crossings except for the purposes of complying with the regulations relating to pelican crossings; or if the driver is prevented from proceeding by circumstances beyond the driver's control; or it is necessary to stop to avoid an accident or to make a left or right turn.

Defences

Defence to Failing to Accord Precedence

The requirement to comply with the regulation is subject to the "principle of impossibility". This means that the offence is not committed if control of the vehicle is taken from the driver in circumstances where the driver is not at fault, for example:
- where the driver is suddenly stung by a swarm of bees;
- where the driver suffers a sudden disability;
- where the vehicle is hit from behind;
- where the vehicle had a latent defect which was unknown to the driver.

Defences to the Stopping Offences

It is a defence for a driver to prove that he or she stopped:
- in circumstances beyond his or her control; or
- to avoid an accident; or
- to allow free passage to pedestrians on the crossing; in other words, to comply with the regulations.

Defence to Overtaking on a Crossing

The offence will not be committed unless the overtaking takes place within the zig-zag lines. If the vehicle being overtaken has entered the black and white stripes of the crossing, the driver who is overtaking will have a defence (although precedence must still be accorded to pedestrians).

Chapter 10

Seat Belts and Protective Headgear

Introduction

The Department of Transport estimates that since the wearing of seat belts in front seats became a legal requirement in 1983, 200 deaths and 7,000 serious injuries have been avoided each year. The importance of the extension of the requirement to back seat passengers has not been widely understood, but according to Department of Transport figures, in a collision at 30 m.p.h., an adult back seat passenger is thrown forward with a force of three and a half tons – equal to the weight of an elephant.

Seat Belts

This offence of not wearing a seat belt may be committed by a driver or a passenger. It is an offence to drive or ride in a "specified motor vehicle" without wearing a seat belt. Only the person contravening the regulation is guilty, and it is not possible to aid and abet or cause or permit this offence. A "specified motor vehicle" means:
- a three wheeled vehicle weighing more than 225 kg;
- a heavy motor car;
- a motor car registered on or after 1 January 1965.

Ordinary cars fall into the category of a motor car registered on or after 1 January 1965.

The driver and a person occupying the "specified passenger's seat" must wear a seat belt when in the vehicle. The "specified passenger's seat" means the front seat beside the driver's seat. If there is more than one such seat, it means the seat furthest from the driver.

Exceptions

The following persons need not wear a seat belt:

- users of vehicles constructed or adapted for the delivery of goods or mail to consumers or addressees, while making local deliveries;
- drivers of vehicles while performing a manoeuvre, which includes reversing;
- any person holding a valid certificate signed by a medical practitioner to the effect that it is inadvisable on medical grounds to wear a seat belt (but see below);
- a qualified driver supervising a provisional licence holder who is reversing;
- taxi drivers;
- drivers of private hire vehicles.

If a person who has a medical certificate is prosecuted for not wearing a seat belt, he or she is not entitled to rely on the exception afforded by the certificate unless:
- it was produced to the constable at the time the driver was informed of possible prosecution; or
- it was produced (1) within seven days after the date on which the driver was so informed; or (2) as soon as is reasonably practicable at such police station as the driver specified to the constable; or
- where it was not produced at a police station, it was not reasonably practicable to produce it there before the day on which the proceedings commenced.

Children under Fourteen

It is an offence without reasonable excuse to drive a motor vehicle on a road with a child under fourteen in the front seat unless the child is wearing a seat belt.

Where a child under fourteen is in the rear of the motor vehicle and a seat belt is fitted in the rear, it is an offence to drive the vehicle without reasonable excuse unless the child is wearing the seat belt.

Where a child under the age of twelve and less than 150 cm in height is:
- in the rear of a passenger car; and
- no seat belt is fitted in the rear of the passenger car; and
- a seat in the front of the passenger car is fitted with a seat belt but is not occupied by a person,

it is an offence without reasonable excuse to drive the passenger on a road. In other words, the child should be in the front wearing the belt unless the front seat is occupied, in which case no offence is committed if no seat belt is fitted in the rear.

An exemption is provided for a child holding a valid certificate signed by a medical practitioner to the effect that it is inadvisable on medical grounds for the child to wear a seat belt. If a driver is prosecuted for this offence, the medical certificate can be relied on only if the conditions set out above, in respect of medical certificates for adult drivers, are met.

It will be a reasonable excuse for the driver to show that he or she had secured the child into the seat belt before commencing the journey but the child released the belt without the driver's knowledge. It will also be a reasonable excuse for the driver to prove that there was insufficient time to secure the seat belt on account of some emergency, such as escaping from an assault.

Rear Seat belts

Where seat belts are fitted in rear seats of a vehicle, both adults and children must wear them.

Penalties

- Driving with a child under fourteen in the rear seat without a seat belt: a fine up to Level 1 on the standard scale;
- driving with a child under fourteen in the front passenger seat without a seat belt, a fine up to Level 2 on the standard scale;
- driving with passengers over the age of fourteen in the rear seats without seat belts: a fine up to Level 2 on the standard scale;
- in any other case, a fine up to Level 2 on the standard scale.

The offences are not endorsable or subject to disqualification.

Protective Headgear

It is an offence to drive or ride a motor cycle without wearing a crash helmet. Only the person committing the contravention is guilty unless he or she is under the age of sixteen, in which case the person who aided and abetted the contravention, as well as the person who is under sixteen, will be liable. For example, John is fifteen and

Geoffrey is sixteen. Both are riding without crash helmets on the same motor cycle; Geoffrey is driving it. Geoffrey is guilty of the offence in relation to himself, and for aiding and abetting John. John is guilty of the offence in relation to himself only.

The offence is not committed by a follower of the Sikh religion while wearing a turban.

Penalties

The maximum fine is up to Level 2 on the standard scale. The offence is not endorsable or subject to disqualification.

Chapter 11

Parking

Local Orders

Minor parking offences are usually contraventions of local orders, and these vary from place to place. For this reason only general guidance on local restrictions can be given here. It may be necessary to examine a local order, which you should be able to find in your public library or local police station. If you cannot obtain a copy of a local order from either of these sources, then your local councillor may be able to help, especially if it is close to election time!

Parking Meters

Local authorities may designate parking places on the highway. Parking time may be purchased by placing coins in the meter. An excess charge is payable if the vehicle remains longer than the time allowed, and parking beyond the time allowed under the excess charge is an offence.

The driver who parked the vehicle is responsible, so if the driver sends someone else to remove the vehicle after the time allowed under the excess charge has expired, the person who parked is liable, not the person who removed the vehicle.

Some local orders require payment immediately the vehicle is parked, so that the driver is not allowed even a few moments to obtain change to place in the meter.

"Feeding" the meter is unlawful even if there was unexpired time on the meter when the vehicle was first parked.

No Waiting

It is an offence to park in a controlled "no waiting" area, but there must be a prescribed "no waiting" sign. If there is no such sign, then you will have a defence.

All parts of a controlled zone, other than parking bays, must be marked with yellow lines. Single yellow lines must be accompanied by a plate specifying the hours of restricted parking. You will have a defence if there is no such plate.

Exemptions from No Waiting Offences

Loading and Unloading

There is an exemption from a "no waiting" restriction for loading and unloading goods not capable of being carried. It is for the driver to prove that he or she was loading or unloading. In decided cases, it has been held that the exemption does not apply to collecting a Chinese take-away meal or to collecting £695 in wages for employees because the items are capable of being carried.

Disabled Persons

All local parking restrictions are subject to exemptions for vehicles displaying an orange disabled person's badge issued by the local authority. The exemptions vary from place to place.

The minimum exemptions provide that for disabled persons there is no charge or time limit at parking meters; no time limit in limited waiting areas; and two hours waiting is permitted in "no waiting" areas. A time disc is issued for use with a disabled person's badge; this must be set and displayed for the exemption to apply.

These are minimum exemptions. Local authorities are empowered to create more liberal exemptions, so it is important to check the local order.

It is an offence wrongfully to use a disabled person's badge. This applies to a person who displays such a badge when not entitled to do so, or when any of the exceptions are exceeded. The offence is punishable by a fine up to Level 3 on the standard scale.

Wheel Clamping

Approved wheel clamping devices may be used to immobilise a vehicle which is illegally parked. A wheel clamp may be fixed only by or under the direction of a constable.

Wheel clamping on private land is lawful provided that the

motorist has seen, and could therefore be taken to have consented to, a notice warning of such consequences. The release fee must be reasonable, easily payable and result in prompt release.

Penalty Charge Notices (Parking Tickets)

Non-endorsable parking offences on residential streets in London boroughs are now dealt with by the local authorities. Elsewhere, prosecutions are conducted by the Central Ticket Office and the system with regard to fixed penalty notices (see page 121) applies. The authority may impose a penalty charge for a parking offence, and if it is not paid, the authority may take action for payment through the county court. It is no longer possible for a driver who disputes having committed a parking offence in London to request a hearing before a magistrates' court. Instead, motorists may make representations to the local authority; if this is unsuccessful, there is a right of appeal to an adjudicator.

A penalty charge notice is issued to the motorist and placed on the vehicle. If the charge is paid within fourteen days, the motorist is given a percentage discount. The percentage varies from area to area.

If the penalty is not paid within 28 days, the authority will obtain information about the registered keeper of the vehicle and send a "notice to owner" to the person who appears to have been the owner of the vehicle when the offence occurred. The notice must:
- state the amount payable;
- state the grounds on which the penalty charge notice was issued;
- state that the penalty charge must be paid within 28 days;
- state that if it is not paid in time, the charge may be increased by 50 per cent;
- state the amount of the increased charge;
- explain the entitlement to make representations to the issuing authority; and
- explain the adjudication process.

The local authority may issue a "charge certificate" if:
- payment has not been received within 28 days of issuing the notice to owner; and
- there have been no representations to the authority; and
- an appeal to the adjudicator has not been made.

A charge certificate increases the penalty charge by 50 per cent. If the charge certificate remains unpaid after fourteen days from the date of service, the authority is entitled to enforce the charge certificate at the county court. Money will then be recovered as if it were under a county court order. The most common method of recovering money is known as "execution against goods". This empowers an enforcement officer to seize and sell goods belonging to the offender to satisfy the debt and the costs of its enforcement. This is usually known as "sending in the bailiffs".

Representations to the issuing authority may be made only after the notice to owner has been issued. Representations may consist of assertions that:
- the recipient was not the owner of the vehicle at the time of the alleged offence;
- the alleged contravention did not occur, for example because the vehicle was being loaded or unloaded; or the penalty charge notice was issued too early; or the vehicle was displaying a valid parking permit, ticket voucher or badge;
- the driver did not have the owner's consent;
- the recipient is a vehicle hire firm and the vehicle was, at the time of the contravention, hired from the firm under a vehicle hiring agreement and the person hiring it had signed a statement acknowledging liability for any penalty charge notice during the period of hire;
- the penalty charge notice exceeds the permitted amount.

Endorsable Parking Offences

Wilful Obstruction of the Free Passage of the Highway

This offence is committed if a person in charge of a motor vehicle or trailer unnecessarily obstructs a road, or causes or permits such an obstruction (see page 19 for the meaning of "causing or permitting").

The obstruction may be of a physical nature, such as blocking the passage of other vehicles, or it may be an unreasonable use of the right to stop, such as undertaking a U-turn in a busy road and thereby holding up other traffic. The obstruction must be of a wilful nature, so that if your vehicle breaks down and so causes an obstruction, you will have a defence as long as you try to remove it within a reasonable time.

Where it is said that a driver made unreasonable use of the right to stop, it is not necessary to show that anyone was actually obstructed. For example, it has been held that ice cream vans and hot dog stalls cause an obstruction because their use of the highway is unreasonable.

Even if you have been granted permission by the local authority to use the highway in a way which is alleged to be unreasonable, this may not be a defence. In one decided case, a man who had sold fruit from the back of a stationary vehicle for many years without any complaint from the local authority was held, on one occasion, to be obstructing the highway. If you are asked to move your vehicle by a police officer because it is causing an obstruction it is always advisable to comply with the request because the police have a power of arrest for obstructing the highway (see page 14).

Leaving a Vehicle in a Dangerous Position

It is an offence to cause or permit a vehicle or trailer to be on a road in such a position, or in such a condition, or in such circumstances, as to involve a danger of injury to other persons.

"In such a position" means, for example, where a vehicle is left parked on a blind corner and an accident is likely to occur. "In such a condition" relates, for example, to cases where a vehicle is left without the handbrake being set.

Penalties

The penalties for the endorsable offences are:
- a fine up to Level 3 on the standard scale;
- obligatory endorsement with three penalty points; and
- discretionary disqualification.

The warning formula (notice of intended prosecution; see page 20) must be given.

Opening the Door of a Motor Vehicle

It is an offence to open or cause or permit a door to be opened so as to injure or endanger any person.

The offence may be committed by the driver or passenger, and parents may be liable for "permitting" the offence if they know that a child is about to open a door. Parents might be liable for "causing" the offence if they instruct a child to open the door.

Defence

It is a defence to take all reasonable precautions to see if traffic is coming.

Penalties

A fine up to Level 4 on the standard scale for goods vehicles but up to Level 3 in respect of other vehicles. The offence is not endorsable nor subject to disqualification.

Chapter 12

Criminal Offences

Introduction

A distinction should be made between motoring offences and criminal offences. Criminal offences are of course more serious. Proceedings for a criminal offence normally commence by arrest and charge rather than by a summons. The police are empowered to take fingerprints, a photograph and a non-intimate sample (ie a sample of hair, nails or saliva, or a footprint) from a person charged with most criminal offences.

Criminal offences dealt with elsewhere in this book include most offences relating to driving and alcohol (Chapter 13), motor manslaughter, dangerous driving and causing death by dangerous driving (Chapter 3). The offences of failing to report an accident and failing to stop after an accident (see Chapter 7) can lead to imprisonment, but are likely to commence by way of a summons.

Taking a Conveyance

The Offence

It is an offence to take unauthorised possession or control of a "conveyance", without the owner's consent or other lawful authority, for one's own use or for another person's use. It is also an offence to drive a conveyance or allow oneself to be carried in or on it knowing that it has been taken without consent.

The offence is one of "taking", not "theft". The legal definition of theft includes an intention to permanently deprive the owner. This element is usually absent when a person takes the conveyance for a "joy ride" and later abandons it. The offence of taking without consent is designed to cover these situations.

The offence is predominantly committed by young persons; two thirds of those convicted of it are under 21.

Note the use of the word "conveyance". The offence is not confined to motor vehicles or mechanically propelled vehicles, but includes any conveyance constructed or adapted for the carriage of persons whether by land, water or air – aircraft, hovercraft, ships, boats and yachts, as well as cars, vans and lorries.

The offence is generally known by its initial letters. In some parts of the country it is known as "TDA", standing for the earlier offence of "taking and driving away", but this is now inaccurate because the offence does not require driving away, but merely taking. In other parts of the country it is rather inelegantly known as TWOC, standing for taking without consent.

"Taking" means taking possession or control contrary to the rights of the owner. There must also be some element of movement.

For the offence to be committed, the conveyance must be taken for the defendant's own use or for the use of another; this means that the conveyance must be used as a form of transport. If a person parks his car in such a way as to block your driveway, you may not be committing the offence if you simply release the handbrake in order to move it out of the way. Similarly, releasing the handbrake of a driverless vehicle will not amount to the offence because the element of control is absent.

In the standard case where a person takes a vehicle which has been parked on the roadway, there is no difficulty in proving that the vehicle was taken without the consent of the owner. Difficulties may arise where the owner gives a person consent to take a conveyance for a particular specified journey, but the conveyance is not returned immediately afterwards and instead is used for another separate journey. The subsequent journey may be without the consent of the owner.

Difficulties may also arise when employees use their employers' vehicles. It seems that the offence will not be committed where an employee takes a vehicle on an unauthorised journey during the course of employment, but it may be committed where the employee takes the vehicle home after work and then uses it for an unauthorised journey.

Passengers may be convicted of taking without consent if they know that the conveyance was taken unlawfully. Alternatively, a passenger may be convicted if it is proved that the passenger was present in the conveyance while it was being used as a conveyance, and that the passenger knew the conveyance had been taken unlawfully.

Defences

It is obviously a defence to show that the owner gave consent. Consent obtained by duress or intimidation is not consent. But where consent was obtained by misrepresentation, the offence is not committed. For example, if it is a precondition of hiring a vehicle that the person hiring it has a driving licence, and the person falsely represents that he or she has a licence, that person does not commit the offence by making false representations, even though the hire company would not have handed over the vehicle had it known the hirer did not have a driving licence.

It is also a defence if the defendant believed that he or she had lawful authority or would have had the owner's consent had the owner known of the circumstances in which the conveyance was taken.

The offence is often accompanied by the offence of having no insurance. Unfortunately for the owner of the vehicle, he or she may be liable for "permitting" the offence of having no insurance by allowing a person who is not covered by insurance to borrow the vehicle.

Penalties

The penalties are:
- six months' imprisonment and/or a fine not exceeding Level 5 on the standard scale;
- compensation up to £5,000;
- the offence is not endorsable but it is subject to discretionary disqualification.

The offence is viewed quite seriously by the courts and the "entry point" (see page 26) is a community penalty (see page 118). Aggravating factors will be if the offence was committed while on bail; more than one person was involved; the offence was premeditated; there was damage; the victim is vulnerable; the defendant has previous convictions and has failed to respond to previous sentences.

A more lenient view will be taken if the keys were left in the conveyance; if there was any misunderstanding with the owner; or if the conveyance was driven only a short distance.

Aggravated Vehicle Taking

This offence was introduced in response to public concern about "joy riders" who drive dangerously or cause injury or damage.

The Offence

Unlike taking without consent, aggravated vehicle taking does not apply to all conveyances, but only to mechanically propelled vehicles.

The offence is committed if:
- the offence of taking without consent (the basic offence) is committed; and
- at any time after the vehicle was taken and before it was recovered:
  - the vehicle was driven dangerously on a road or other public place. "Dangerous" has the same meaning as in "dangerous driving" (see page 45);
  - owing to the driving of the vehicle, an accident occurred causing injury to any person.
  - owing to the driving of the vehicle, an accident occurred causing damage to any property other than the vehicle.
  - damage was caused to the vehicle *after* it was taken. The offence is not committed if damage is caused to the vehicle in order to take it.

The offence may be committed by a passenger as well as by the driver.

Defences

It is necessary for the prosecution to prove the basic offence of taking without consent, and so the defences to that offence (see above) are available to someone charged with the aggravated offence.

It is also a defence to prove that the driving, injury or damage occurred before the basic offence was committed; or that the defendant was not in or on, or in the immediate vicinity of, the vehicle when the driving, injury or damage occurred.

Penalties

The offence is triable either at the magistrates' court or at the Crown Court. The maximum penalty in the magistrates' court is six months' imprisonment and/or a fine not exceeding Level 5 on the standard scale. In the Crown Court, the maximum penalty is two years' imprisonment and/or an unlimited fine, except where the accident caused the death of a person, in which case the maximum term of imprisonment is five years. Endorsement is obligatory with three to eleven points, and disqualification for a minimum of twelve months is automatic. The "entry point" for sentencing (see page 26) is a term of imprisonment.

The court will regard the following as aggravating features: the fact that the vehicle was driven dangerously; the extent of physical harm done; the length of time the vehicle was driven; whether the offence was committed while on bail; whether there was any attempt to avoid detection or apprehension; competitive driving, racing or showing off; disregard of warnings, for example from passengers or others in the vicinity; excessive speed; evidence of alcohol or drugs; group action; premeditation; serious injury or damage; serious risk; previous convictions and failures to respond to previous sentences.

Mitigating factors will include cases where the keys were left in the car; the absence of alcohol or drugs; minor damage; a single incident; and where speed was not excessive.

Interfering with a Motor Vehicle

The Offence

This offence was introduced to deal with people who "try car door handles" but are caught before they steal or take away the car, or steal from it.

It is an offence to interfere with a motor vehicle or trailer with the intention to commit, either alone or with another person, the offences of:
- theft of the motor vehicle or trailer or part of it; or
- theft of anything carried in or on the motor vehicle or trailer; or
- taking without consent.

It is not necessary for the prosecution to prove which one of these offences was intended.

Penalties

The maximum penalty is three months' imprisonment or a fine up to Level 4 on the standard scale; an offender's licence is not endorsable for this offence; nor is the offender liable to disqualification.

Driving Whilst Disqualified

A driver may be disqualified either because he commits an offence subject to obligatory or discretionary disqualification (see page 126), or because he is a "totter" (see page 127).

The Offence

It is an offence for a person who is disqualified from holding or obtaining a licence to drive a motor vehicle on the road. The offence applies only to motor vehicles and only to roads rather than other public places.

The offence is one of strict liability (see page 22) and it is no defence to say that you did not believe that you were disqualified or you thought your term of disqualification had expired. Nor is it a defence to say that you had to drive in an emergency – although the defence of necessity (ie that the offence was committed in order to save life or limb) may be open to a defendant, but only in extreme circumstances. In one decided case, a man drove while disqualified because his wife had threatened to commit suicide if he did not drive their son to work. His wife had a history of suicide attempts and the court decided that this was a relevant factor.

A constable in uniform has the power to arrest without warrant any person who is driving a motor vehicle on a road if he has reasonable grounds to suspect that the person is disqualified.

Penalties

The consequences of driving while disqualified are:
- obligatory endorsement with six points;
- discretionary disqualification;
- six months' imprisonment or a fine up to Level 5 on the standard

scale.

The "entry point" (see page 26) for sentencing is custody. The court will have regard to the following aggravating factors: that the offence was committed on bail; that the offender made efforts to avoid detection; that the distance driven was long; that there was planned long term evasion; that the disqualification was recently imposed; that there are previous convictions and failures to respond to previous sentences; and repeated offences over a short period of time.

The court will also take into account the following mitigating factors: that there was an emergency; or that the distance driven was short.

Obtaining a Driving Licence While Disqualified

It is an offence for a person who is disqualified to obtain a driving licence.

Penalties

The penalty is a fine up to Level 3 on the standard scale; the licence may not be endorsed; and the defendant is not subject to disqualification.

After the Disqualification Period

If you have been disqualified, you will need to apply to the Driver and Vehicle Licensing Authority for the return of your licence after the period of disqualification has ended. If you drive after the disqualification period has ended and have not applied for a licence, you will committing the offence of driving otherwise than in accordance with a driving licence (see page 39).

If you have held a licence in the past and are entitled to hold a licence after the period of disqualification, you are entitled to drive after the disqualification period has ended even if you are not in physical possession of a licence, but you must still apply for the return of your licence. Application forms are available from most Post Offices.

Fraudulent Use of a Vehicle Excise Licence

It is an offence to forge, fraudulently alter, use, lend or allow to be used by another person a vehicle excise licence (or "tax disc"). The most common way in which this offence is committed is by displaying the vehicle excise licence for one vehicle on another vehicle. An excise licence has written on it the registration number of the vehicle for which it was issued and must not be used for any other vehicle.

It is not necessary for the prosecution to prove that there was intent to avoid payment of the fee – merely that there was an intent to deceive. But it is necessary for the prosecution to prove that the defendant acted dishonestly.

Penalties

The offence is triable either in the magistrates' court or in the Crown Court. In the magistrates' court, the maximum penalty is a fine of £2,000, and in the Crown Court the maximum sentence is two years imprisonment, an unlimited fine or both. The offence does not attract endorsement or disqualification.

Causing Danger to Road Users

This offence is intended to cover those situations where a person deliberately does something to obstruct traffic and which has the result that danger is caused. It is not necessary for the prosecution to prove an intention to cause danger. What must be proved is that the act itself was intentional. So, it is an offence if a person intentionally and without lawful authority or reasonable excuse:
- causes anything to be on or over a road; or
- interferes with a motor vehicle, trailer or cycle; or
- interferes (directly or indirectly) with traffic equipment

in such circumstances that it would be obvious to a reasonable person that to do so would be dangerous.

The offence covers deliberate obstruction of the road and such acts as interfering with the braking, steering or tyres of a vehicle; or interfering with traffic signs or signals, for example by turning round a "one way street" sign so that the arrow points the wrong way.

"Danger" means danger of injury to any person while on or near the road, or serious damage to property on or near the road.

Penalties

The offence is triable in either the magistrates' court or the Crown Court. In the magistrates' court the maximum penalty is six months' imprisonment and/or a fine up to the maximum £5,000. In the Crown Court, the maximum is seven years' imprisonment and/or an unlimited fine.

Chapter 13

Alcohol and Drugs

Introduction

Alcohol is a major contributor to road accidents and it is estimated that nearly one in five of all deaths on the road may be attributed to alcohol.

Because of its familiarity we sometimes overlook the fact that alcohol is a drug and exerts powerful effects on the body. It is a depressant which slows down the processes of the higher centres of the brain. It impairs driving ability because it affects inhibition, judgement, coordination and emotional reaction.

Alcoholic drink passes quickly from the mouth to the stomach and then into the small intestine. From the upper part of the small intestine (the duodenum) it passes into the blood stream and is distributed to those tissues which contain water, including the brain.

Alcohol is eliminated by the liver, but the process is slow.

Even after a person has finished drinking, alcohol continues to be absorbed into the blood stream from the duodenum, and the concentration of alcohol in the blood rises more quickly than the liver can eliminate it. That is why a driver may still be above the legal limit several hours after his or her last drink.

Blood Alcohol Concentration

The amount of alcohol in the blood is affected by:
- the type of drink consumed;
- the period of time over which the drinks were consumed;
- stomach contents; and
- body weight.

Type of Drink
Some alcoholic drinks are more rapidly absorbed than others. Those that are 20 per cent alcohol by volume, such as equal proportions of whisky and water or neat sherry, are most quickly absorbed. Strong solutions of alcohol delay the opening of the valve between the stomach and duodenum and are slowly absorbed. Beer is slowly absorbed because the alcohol in it takes times to pass through the volume of liquid before reaching the intestinal walls. If a drink is carbonated, the rate at which alcohol is absorbed into the blood is slightly increased.

Time
Alcohol consumed over a short period is absorbed more quickly than the liver can eliminate it.

Stomach Contents
If there is no food in the stomach, alcohol will come into contact with the stomach walls, and so be absorbed, relatively quickly. Food, particularly fatty food, impedes the absorption of alcohol through the stomach walls.

Body Weight
Since two thirds of the body is water, large people have more water in their bodies than small people. Alcohol is absorbed by this water, and therefore a large person will have a lower blood-alcohol concentration than a small person who has drunk an equal amount. Alcohol is less soluble in fat than in water, so a fat person will reach a higher blood-alcohol concentration than a muscular person of the same weight who has consumed the same quantity of alcohol (other factors being equal).

Measuring Blood-Alcohol Concentration
Blood carries alcohol to the lungs and, because alcohol is a volatile drug, a small proportion of it evaporates from the blood into the breath. Machines which measure breath-alcohol concentration therefore also measure blood-alcohol concentration. Only deep lung air makes contact with the blood so the concentration of alcohol in a person's body can be measured only from deep lung air. How the

breath analysis machines work is described at the end of this chapter.

Drugs

It is not only illegal drugs such as heroin, cocaine and cannabis that impair driving ability. Commonly prescribed drugs, such as tranquillisers, sedatives and anti-depressants, also have a negative effect on driving ability. Many hay fever remedies contain an antihistamine such as promethazine hydrochloride, which also has a negative effect on driving. Many over-the-counter remedies for influenza and colds contain both an antihistamine and a quantity of alcohol.

An Outline of the Drink-Drive Law

A police officer in uniform may require a person to provide a breath test if the officer has reasonable cause to suspect that the person:
 – has been or is driving a motor vehicle with alcohol in his or her body;
 – has been or is "in charge" of a motor vehicle, with alcohol in his or her body; or
 – has committed a moving traffic offence. A "moving traffic offence" covers most traffic offences.

An officer may not, however, require a specimen from a person who is in hospital as a patient.

Where there has been a road traffic accident, a police officer, not necessarily in uniform, may require a person to take a breath test if the officer has reasonable cause to believe that the person was driving, or attempting to drive, or was "in charge" of, the vehicle at the time of the accident. Note that here the constable need only have reasonable cause to "believe" (rather than to "suspect", as above). Again, there is an exception for hospital patients.

A person who provides a positive breath test may be arrested. A person who fails to provide a breath test and does not have a reasonable excuse may also be arrested.

A police officer may arrest a person if the officer has reasonable cause to suspect that the person is or has been driving whilst unfit to drive through drink or drugs.

When investigating whether a person has driven or attempted to drive, or been in charge of a motor vehicle, with excess alcohol or whilst unfit through drink or drugs, a police officer may require the person to provide two specimens of breath for analysis. In certain circumstances, blood or urine may be required instead of breath.

A person who provides a positive specimen, or fails without reasonable excuse to provide specimens, is guilty of an offence.

A person who is unfit to drive through drink or drugs is guilty of an offence.

A person who causes death by careless driving or without reasonable consideration for other road users whilst under the influence of drink or drugs is guilty of an offence.

In this chapter we shall therefore be considering the following offences:
- failing to provide a breath test (the roadside screening test);
- driving or attempting to drive a motor vehicle with excess alcohol in the breath, blood or urine;
- driving or attempting to drive a mechanically propelled vehicle whilst unfit through drink or drugs;
- being in charge of a mechanically propelled vehicle whilst unfit through drink or drugs;
- being in charge of a mechanically propelled vehicle with excess alcohol in the breath, blood or urine or whilst unfit through drink or drugs;
- failing to provide a specimen of breath, blood or urine for analysis;
- causing death by careless driving or without reasonable consideration whilst under the influence of drink or drugs.

Powers of Arrest

A police officer may arrest a person without warrant if:
- as a result of a breath test the officer has reasonable cause to suspect that the proportion of alcohol in the person's breath exceeds the prescribed limit;
- the suspect has failed to provide a specimen of breath when required to do so and the officer has reasonable cause to suspect that the person has alcohol in his or her body;
- the officer has reasonable cause to suspect that the person is or has been committing an offence of driving whilst unfit through drink or drugs.

Powers of Entry

A police officer has a power of entry, if necessary by force, into any place where a person is or where the officer, with reasonable cause, suspects the person to be:
- to arrest the person where the officer has reasonable cause to suspect that the person was driving or in charge whilst unfit; or
- to require the person to provide a specimen of breath for a screening test; or
- to arrest the person for failure to provide a screening test or for providing a positive screening test where:
    (a) an accident has occurred owing to the presence of a motor vehicle on a road or other public place, and
    (b) the officer has reasonable cause to suspect that the accident involved injury to another person.

The Screening or Preliminary or Roadside Breath Test

This is a preliminary test for the purpose of obtaining an indication whether the proportion of alcohol in a person's breath, blood or urine is likely to exceed the prescribed limit.

The device used for this test is a small hand-held machine with a mouthpiece attached (the "breathalyser"). The police may use any one of five approved devices, but the most common is known as the Lion Alcometer SL 2. Because of the effect of mouth alcohol, the device should not be used within twenty minutes of taking one's last drink. The officer may require you to wait for twenty minutes before taking the test. Once you have blown into the mouthpiece the device will indicate whether you are above or below the limit. If the light turns to red, this is a positive reading. If the light turns to red and amber, or amber alone, or green alone, this is a negative result. One continuous breath is required to bring on the light.

As already noted, the police can require a roadside breath test if they suspect a moving traffic offence has been committed. Random testing is not allowed, but the police may stop vehicles at random, and if they then suspect that the motorist has alcohol in his or her body, may require a breath test.

Where there has been an accident on a road or other public place, a constable, not necessarily in uniform, may require any person whom the officer has reasonable cause to believe was driving or attempting to drive, or was in charge of a vehicle at the time of the accident, to provide a specimen of breath for a breath test. The exception for hospital patients applies.

There must actually have been an accident; it is not enough that the officer has reasonable cause to believe that there was one. There must also be a causal connection between the vehicle in question and the accident. Put another way, vehicle A need not be physically involved in the accident but there must be some connection between its presence on the road and the accident, as where the driver of car A brakes suddenly causing car B to collide with car C. On the other hand, there is an insufficient connection where, for example, a pedestrian runs across the road to avoid a car and runs into and injures another pedestrian.

If a vehicle runs off the road because of bad driving, this is still an accident owing to the presence of the vehicle on a road for these purposes.

Failing to provide a breath test without a reasonable excuse is an offence. At this stage, the officer need not warn the motorist that failure to provide a specimen may result in prosecution.

If the driver or person in charge provides a positive test or fails without reasonable excuse to provide a specimen, he or she may be arrested.

This leads to the next offence which we shall consider, which is driving or attempting to drive with excess alcohol.

Driving or Attempting to Drive with Excess Alcohol

It is an offence to drive or attempt to drive a motor vehicle on a road or other public place after consuming so much alcohol that the proportion of it in the breath, blood or urine exceeds the prescribed limit.

"Consuming" is not limited to drinking, and a driver may still be guilty of the offence if medication which contains alcohol has been given by intravenous injection.

The prescribed limit is 35 microgrammes of alcohol in 100 millilitres of breath, or 80 milligrammes of alcohol in 100 millilitres of blood, or 107 milligrammes of alcohol in 100 millilitres of urine.

The following European countries have the same prescribed limit as this country: Austria, Belgium, Denmark, France, Germany, Italy and Spain. In Czechoslovakia, Turkey and Hungary, it is an offence to drive with any alcohol at all in one's breath, blood or urine. In Poland and Sweden the prescribed limit is 20 milligrammes in blood or 8 microgrammes in breath. In Finland and Greece the limit is 50 milligrammes in blood or 22 microgrammes in breath. In the Republic of Ireland the limit is 100 milligrammes in blood or 43 microgrammes in breath.

Once a motorist has been arrested, either for providing a positive breath test or for failing without reasonable excuse to provide a breath test, the motorist is usually required to provide a specimen of breath rather than blood or urine.

There are two approved devices for analysing breath samples. These are the Lion Intoximeter 3000 which is used in most of the country, and the Camic Breath Analyser which is used in the North of England and in Scotland.

Before being asked to provide specimens, the officer will normally ask the following questions:
– When did you last have an alcoholic drink?
– Have you used a mouth wash or spray in the last twenty minutes?
– Have you smoked in the last five minutes?

Many mouth washes and sprays contain alcohol. Cigarette smoke contains acetone.

The officer must warn that failure to provide specimens will render you liable to prosecution. The officer will require two specimens of breath but must tell you that the higher reading will be disregarded. The result of the analysis will be shown on a printout. You will be offered a copy of the printout and asked to sign it. If it is not handed to you at the time, it must be served on you not less than seven days before the court hearing. You are entitled to object to the production of the printout if, not later than three days before the hearing, or within such other time as the court allows, you notify the prosecution that you require the person who signed the printout to attend court. You may wish to object to the production of the printout if you are a diabetic and the printout shows no deduction for an acetone reading (see page 117), or where the printout shows an excess alcohol reading but you have not consumed alcohol and you suspect the machine to be faulty. It is advisable to object to the production of the printout where the difference between the two readings is more than 20 per cent; this may be an indication that the machine is not working properly.

It is presumed that the breath, blood or urine alcohol level at the time of the alleged offence was no lower than at the time the specimen was provided. This means that the driver cannot later try to show that at the time of the alleged offence the alcohol reading would have been lower than at the time the specimen was provided. The prosecution, on the other hand, is entitled to make a back calculation to show that the alcohol reading at the time of the offence was higher than at the time the specimen was provided.

Specimen of Blood or Urine

If the specimen with the lower proportion of alcohol contains no more than 50 microgrammes, the motorist who provided it may claim that it should be replaced by a specimen of blood or urine. If such a specimen is provided, then neither specimen of breath may be used.

The police may ask you to provide a specimen of blood or urine rather than breath in the following circumstances:

- if the officer has reasonable cause to believe that for medical reasons a specimen of breath cannot be provided or should not be required; or
- at the time the requirement is made an analysis device, or reliable analysis device, is not available at the police station or, for any other reason, it is not practicable to use it there, as where, for example, no trained operator is present at the police station; or
- you are suspected of driving whilst unfit and the officer has been advised by a doctor that the unfitness may be due to a drug.

It is important to note that the requirement for blood, breath or urine may be made during an investigation into whether a person has committed an offence of driving with excess alcohol or driving whilst unfit. You must therefore provide the specimens when required to do so, even if you were not the driver of the vehicle. Where more than one person was present in a motor vehicle and the police do not know who was driving, all of them may be required to provide specimens as long as there are reasonable grounds to suspect or believe that each has alcohol in his or her body.

The police will decide whether the specimen will be of blood or urine. If the officer decides that the specimen should be one of blood, your only ground for objecting to blood and asking for a urine specimen to be provided instead is medical reasons. There is no obligation on the police to invite a driver to express a preference.

Two specimens of urine must be provided within one hour of being required. Only the second is used for analysis. This provides a safeguard for the motorist since the first sample is likely to contain an unrepresentatively high proportion of alcohol.

A person supplies a specimen of blood if and only if he consents to its being taken by a medical practitioner and it is so taken. A specimen of blood is to be disregarded unless it is taken with the consent of the accused and by a medical practitioner. If a doctor takes a specimen of blood without consent, the doctor may be liable for assault.

There is no obligation on the police to supply part of the specimen to the driver unless the driver asks for it. If you do, you will be given a part of the sample of blood or urine in a suitable container. Evidence of the proportion of alcohol or drugs found in the specimen cannot then be used by the prosecution unless:
- the specimen the prosecution uses is one of two parts into which the specimen was divided at the time it was provided; and
- the other part was supplied to the defendant.

The normal procedure for supplying specimens of blood or urine to the driver is known as the "brown envelope" procedure. The specimen is placed in a sealed envelope which is normally signed on the seal by the officer. The envelope is marked with the following precautions:
- Do not open the envelope;
- Send it without delay for analysis;
- Keep it in the refrigerator;
- Pack it strongly and send by post.

The back of the envelope also contains information that a list of analysts may be obtained from the police station or from the Royal Society of Chemists.

The reason a motorist might ask for a sample of the blood or urine is to obtain a private analysis. Sometimes the prosecution analysis shows the blood or urine alcohol level to be above the prescribed limit while the private analysis shows it to be below the level. For this reason, it is advisable to obtain a private analysis, although you will have to pay for it.

Even after you have been charged with the offence of excess alcohol the police may detain you at the police station until it appears that, if you are released, you would not be committing a further offence of driving with excess alcohol or whilst unfit to drive. The police may not detain you if there is no likelihood of your driving. If your ability to drive is impaired through drugs, the officer must act on the advice of a medical practitioner.

Defence

It is a defence to a charge of driving with excess alcohol to prove:
- that the driver consumed alcohol after he or she had ceased driving or attempting to drive the vehicle; and
- that otherwise, the proportion of alcohol in the blood, breath or urine would not have exceeded the prescribed limit. The onus is on the defendant, on the balance of probabilities (ie that it is more likely than not that the proportion of alcohol would not have exceeded the prescribed limit). To prove this defence, you will need to call expert evidence. The expert will calculate what your alcohol concentration in blood, breath or urine would have been had you not consumed alcohol after driving. This is normally calculated by means of the "Widmark formula" which is:

$$C = \frac{A}{p \times r}$$

C = the peak concentration in blood; A = the amount of alcohol in grammes; p = the weight of the driver in kilogrammes; r = the Widmark factor, ie 0.68 for men and 0.55 for women.

Driving Whilst Unfit

It is an offence to drive or attempt to drive a mechanically propelled vehicle on a road or other public place while unfit to drive through drink or drugs. A person is taken to be unfit to drive if his or her ability to drive is for the time being impaired. Where a person provides a specimen which proves to be above the prescribed limit, the charge will usually be one of driving with excess alcohol. The alternative charge of driving whilst unfit is usually brought where:

- the impairment is due to a drug; or
- the person has failed to provide a specimen and the police suspect the person is unfit to drive, in which case both offences – driving whilst unfit and failing to provide a specimen (see page 108) – are likely to be charged.

Impairment may be proved by:
- the manner of driving, accompanied by evidence of drink or drugs;
- evidence from the police that the driver's eyes were glazed; the driver's speech was slurred; the driver's breath smelt of intoxicating liquor and the driver was unsteady on his or her feet.
- a non-expert witness may give evidence about whether, in his or her opinion, the person had been drinking, but not whether the person was fit to drive.
- by a doctor's examination with the driver's consent. The doctor will usually conduct a number of tests, including the Rhomberg test which measures steadiness on one's feet, and the Nystagmus test, which measures eye movement.

"Drug" means any intoxicant other than alcohol and includes prescription-only medicines as well as over-the-counter medicines, and solvents.

If your condition is suspected to be due to a drug rather than alcohol, you may be required to provide a blood or urine specimen because the breath analysis machines measure the concentration of alcohol, rather than of any other substance.

In Charge Whilst Unfit or With Excess Alcohol

It is an offence to be in charge of a mechanically propelled vehicle on a road or other public place whilst unfit through drink or drugs or after consuming so much alcohol that the proportion in a person's breath, blood or urine exceeds the prescribed limit. A person may still be in charge of a vehicle even when several miles away from it. The normal test of whether a person is in charge is whether the person is in possession of the keys. The lawful possessor of a motor vehicle, or the person who placed a vehicle on the road, is normally considered to be in charge until he or she relinquishes control.

Defence

A person is considered not to have been in charge of a motor vehicle if it is proved that at the material time there was no likelihood of driving it so long as the person remained unfit to drive through drink or drugs. Expert evidence may be necessary.

Defence to In Charge With Excess Alcohol

It is a defence for a person charged with being in charge with excess alcohol to prove that at the time there was no likelihood of driving the vehicle whilst the proportion of alcohol in his or her breath, blood or urine remained likely to exceed the prescribed limit. Expert evidence is normally required to establish this defence.

Special Protection for a Hospital Patient

The power of the police to arrest a person is suspended while the person is at a hospital as a patient. While a suspect is at a hospital as a patient, the medical practitioner in immediate charge of the case must be notified before the suspect is required to provide a breath test or specimens of blood or urine for analysis.

A breath specimen for analysis cannot be taken at a hospital, but only at a police station. The officer must tell a hospital patient that a breath specimen cannot be taken and must ask if there is any reason why a specimen of blood should not be taken.

The protection applies only to a person who is in hospital as a patient, and so does not apply after a person has been discharged, even if still on hospital premises.

Failing to Provide a Specimen

A person who, without reasonable excuse, fails to provide a specimen of breath when required to do so is guilty of an offence.

There must be an act constituting failure, for example a positive refusal or an insufficient specimen to enable a test or analysis to be carried out.

The specimen must be provided in such a way as to enable the objective of the analysis to be satisfactorily achieved. If you fail to blow hard enough, you may be liable for the offence of failing to provide a specimen.

If you have a medical condition which prevents you giving breath you should say so at the time the requirement is made. The officer then has power to require blood or urine.

You have no right to require or insist that conditions be attached to giving a specimen. Agreeing to provide a specimen only if a solicitor or diplomat is present amounts to a refusal.

Reasonable Excuse

"Reasonable excuses" are normally confined to:
- medical reasons, ie:
    (a) that a person is physically or medically unable to provide a specimen; or
    (b) that its provision will entail a substantial risk to health; or
- that the person did not understand the requirement because, for example, his or her understanding of English was limited.

Trying one's hardest is no defence.

Asthma, bronchitis and sinusitis may amount to a reasonable excuse, but if you are merely suffering from a cold and find it difficult to breathe through the nose, this will not be an acceptable excuse.

It is no defence to say that you were too drunk to provide a specimen. However, in certain extreme circumstances, intoxication may be a medical reason for requiring blood or urine instead of breath. The fact that you are shocked or embarrassed at being in the police station is not a reasonable excuse.

A fear of needles is not normally a reasonable excuse for failing to provide blood, but it may be if it amounts to a phobia.

Several people have unsuccessfully put forward the defence of reasonable excuse on the basis that they feared contracting AIDS either through the mouthpiece on the breath analysis machine or through the use of syringes. This defence was successfully argued in one decided case, but only on the ground that the man in question had a *phobia* of contracting AIDS, to the extent that he took his own beer glass when he went to the pub.

It is no defence to say that you were not the driver or that you have not committed a moving traffic offence, or even that the police were acting in bad faith.

A religious belief prohibiting the giving of blood has been held not to be a reasonable excuse.

It is not a reasonable excuse that you wish to see a solicitor and take legal advice before providing a specimen.

Disqualification

A person convicted of driving or attempting to drive with excess alcohol or driving whilst unfit is liable to obligatory disqualification for not less than twelve months. On a second conviction for an alcohol-related offence within ten years, disqualification is for not less than three years. The ten years run from the date of conviction for the first offence to the commission of the second offence.

Special Reasons for Not Disqualifying

The only way to avoid disqualification is to prove that there are special reasons for not disqualifying.

Even if special reasons are found, it does not follow that the driver will not be disqualified. Even if the court finds that a special reason exists, it will then consider whether there are clear and compelling reasons for exercising its discretion in favour of the motorist. It is rare to do so where there was a high reading.

The special reasons must relate to the *offence* and not the offender. Therefore the following are not special reasons:
- disability;
- a defective liver that destroys alcohol more slowly than in normal people;
- that you are a professional driver or have a good driving record or that disqualification will cause serious hardship;
- ignorance of the overnight effects of alcohol;
- a low level of alcohol.

Again because the special reasons must relate to the offence rather than the offender, they are confined to the following circumstances:
- the shortness of distance driven;
- emergencies;
- laced drinks.

The Shortness of Distance Driven

This argument is sometimes put forward where a person parks a car before entering a public house with no intention of driving afterwards, but, upon leaving the public house considers that the car is in an unsafe position or vulnerable to theft, and decides to move it a short distance to park it elsewhere. It rarely succeeds because the court will always consider the manner of driving; the condition of the vehicle; how far the driver intended to travel; the road and traffic conditions; the possibility of contact with other road users; and the reason the vehicle was driven. The most important of these considerations is the possibility of contact with other road users.

Emergencies

An emergency may amount to a special reason but only in respect of the journey which was the immediate result of the emergency. The return journey will not count as an emergency. For example, in one decided case, a driver had to take a passenger with a leaking colostomy bag to hospital. He was stopped on the return journey and it was held that he no longer had a special reason for not being disqualified, as the emergency was over. The courts will also consider whether the driver has acted responsibly; whether the driver had intended not to drive but was confronted with an emergency situation; whether the driver did everything possible to avoid driving, for example seeking other means of transport such as a taxi; the manner of driving; and the proportion of alcohol in the breath, blood or urine.

Some examples of successfully argued cases on emergency are:
- a man was blackmailed into driving by a woman who threatened to cry rape;
- the steward of a golf club was called to a burglary at the club and asked by the police to drive his car across the doorway to block the burglar's exit.
- a young man and his friends were caught up in a serious disturbance and his friends suffered head injuries. No ambulance was available because of the disturbances and, for the same reason, the local taxi company refused to go out. It was only then that the driver decided to take his friends to hospital by car;
- a female driver had driven to a public house with no intention of driving home. She received a call from her baby-sitter that the baby's father was making threats to the child and to the baby-sitter. She tried to get a taxi by telephone but was unable to do so and tried to find other means of transport. She then drove herself home.

It should be noted that in the last two cases the alcohol reading was low.

An example of an unsuccessful argument on the grounds of emergency is a driver who went to her former boyfriend's home where she was assaulted and her car damaged. She drove to a friend's house and phoned the police, and asked them to meet her at home. She then drank some brandy and drove home. She failed in her argument for special reasons because the emergency arose before she made her decision to drink.

Laced Drinks
This special reason arises where either a drink was actively laced, or was stronger than the driver believed it to be, especially if the driver was misled.

It will be necessary for the defendant to prove that the drink was laced; that the defendant had no knowledge or suspicion of this fact; and that if it had not been laced the defendant would not have been above the limit. Expert evidence will normally be required. An expert witness normally uses the Widmark factor (see page 106). Even if your drink has been laced, the court will consider whether you should have realised that you were unfit, and whether you should have realised that the drink had been laced.

If the lacing should have been detectable, then the court may find special reasons, but still decide to disqualify the driver. In a decided case, the defendant asked for alcohol-free wine but was given wine of normal strength. He left a hospitality tent in which he had been drinking, got into his car and immediately drove into a hedge. The reading was 99 in breath; it was held that although there were special reasons, he should have known that he was drinking normal strength wine and should not therefore have driven.

Causing Death by Careless Driving when Under the Influence of Drink or Drugs

It is an offence if a person causes the death of another person by driving a mechanically propelled vehicle on a road or other public place without due care and attention or without reasonable consideration for other persons using the road or public place, and the driver:

- is at the time of driving unfit to drive through drink or drugs; or
- has consumed so much alcohol that the proportion of it in the blood, breath or urine at that time exceeds the prescribed limit; or
- is, within 18 hours after that time, required to provide a specimen but without reasonable excuse fails to do so.

Penalties

Driving or Attempting to Drive with Excess Alcohol

- Up to six months' imprisonment or a fine up to Level 5 on the standard scale;
- obligatory endorsement with three to eleven points if there are special reasons for not disqualifying;
- obligatory disqualification for a minimum of twelve months.

The court must disqualify for this offence unless special reasons are found. Twelve months is the minimum disqualification, but see page 110 regarding longer periods of disqualification for a second or subsequent conviction within ten years. Magistrates are advised to disqualify for fourteen months if the reading is 61 or above; 16 months if the reading is 65 or above; 20 months if the reading is 78 or above; and 24 months if the reading is 91 or above.

For readings of 70 or above the court will consider a sentence of imprisonment, although in 1993 only five per cent of persons convicted of excess alcohol were sentenced to imprisonment.

The court will view the offence seriously where the offender has a previous conviction for a similar offence, especially if the previous offence was recent. If you find yourself in this position, it is recommended you seek legal advice.

In Charge Whilst Unfit or with Excess Alcohol

- Up to three months' imprisonment and/or a fine up to Level 4 on the standard scale;
- obligatory endorsement with ten penalty points;
- discretionary disqualification.

Driving Whilst Unfit through Drink or Drugs

The penalties are the same as for driving or attempting to drive with excess alcohol.

Failing to Provide a Specimen for the Screening Device
- A fine up to Level 3 on the standard scale;
- obligatory endorsement with four penalty points;
- discretionary disqualification.

Failing to Provide a Specimen for the Evidential Breath Machine or Failing to Provide a Specimen of Blood or Urine if Driving or Attempting to Drive
- Up to six months' imprisonment or a fine up to Level 5 on the standard scale;
- obligatory endorsement with a minimum of twelve months;
- if there are special reasons for not disqualifying, then obligatory endorsement with ten penalty points.

Although the minimum disqualification is for twelve months, the court will usually take a serious view of failing to provide a specimen, and the starting point will often be eighteen months disqualification.

Failing to Provide a Specimen for the Screening Device or Failing to Provide a Specimen of Blood or Urine if in Charge
- Imprisonment for up to three months or a fine up to Level 4 on the standard scale;
- obligatory endorsement with ten penalty points;
- discretionary disqualification.

Causing Death by Careless Driving when under the Influence of Drink or Drugs
- A maximum of ten years' imprisonment;
- obligatory disqualification for a minimum period of two years;
- obligatory endorsement with three to eleven penalty points if there are special reasons of not disqualifying.

A prison sentence is normally considered appropriate for this offence. Its length depends on aggravating and mitigating factors, especially the degree of carelessness and the amount of alcohol. A non-custodial sentence may be justified in exceptional cases where the driver is just over the limit and there has been momentary carelessness with strong mitigation. More than one death is an aggravating factor. In bad cases, such as racing or reckless disregard for the safety of others, a sentence of five years or more is justified. In the worst of contested cases, a sentence of up to ten years is justified. The prime concern of the court is the criminality of the offender, but the court will also have regard to the consequences. Personal elements of mitigation will not deflect the court from passing a sentence appropriate to the gravity of the offence.

Removal or Reduction of Period of Disqualification

Removal

A person who has been disqualified may apply to the court which imposed the disqualification to remove it.

When considering such an application, the court will have regard to:
- the character of the person disqualified and his or her conduct since the order;
- the nature of the offence; and
- any other circumstances of the case.

The court may remove the disqualification from such date as may be specified, or refuse the application.

No application for the removal of disqualification may be made before the expiration of:
- two years from the date of disqualification if the disqualification is for less than four years;
- one half of the period of disqualification if it is for less than ten years but not less than four years;
- five years in any other case.

Where an application for removal has been refused, a further application may not be made for three months.

The court is less likely to remove a mandatory disqualification than a discretionary one.

The court is most likely to remove a disqualification where the person:
- has not committed any offence since the disqualification was ordered;
- has been offered employment which requires the person to drive;

- has, since the time of the order, developed an illness or disability which makes the use of public transport difficult;
- can produce medical evidence that the person has overcome addiction to drink or drugs.

Reduction of Period

Persons disqualified for drink driving offences, including death by dangerous driving, may have their periods of disqualification reduced by completing a rehabilitation course. The reduction will be not less than three months and not more than a quarter of the length of disqualification.

The scheme is voluntary and at present is available only in a few parts of the country. The disqualified person must apply to the court for an order that the period of disqualification be reduced on completion of the course. The conditions which must be satisfied are as follows:
- there must be a place available on a course;
- the offender must be over the age of seventeen;
- the court must explain the effect of the order, the cost and the requirements of the course; and
- the offender must consent to the order.

Courses give information about drink and its effect on the human body; the effect of alcohol on driving ability; analysis of drink-driving offences and preventing future offences.

Operating Principles of the Breath Analysis Machines

The Lion Intoximeter

The Lion Intoximeter absorbs infra-red light to quantify the alcohol concentration in the breath of the subject using the device. It applies an infra-red light source and an infra-red light detector which are connected by a chamber through which breath passes. The stronger the breath-alcohol concentration the less light is able to reach the detector.

The wave length is set at 3.8 microns (a micron is one millionth of a metre) because alcohol vapour absorbs infra-red light most strongly at this wave length.

3.8 microns is also the wave length at which acetone is most strongly absorbed. The Lion Intoximeter has an acetone detector which deducts the acetone reading from the alcohol reading. Acetone is most commonly found in the breath of persons suffering from diabetes but may also be found in the breath of those who are fasting or are on high carbohydrate diets.

You will be asked to blow continuously through a mouthpiece until a series of bars is lit on the display panel. The device will abort if the subject does not blow hard or continuously enough for two or three bars to be lit. The device is set so as to allow three minutes in which to provide a sample, and up to five attempts may be made within that time before the device will register "no sample".

The device is calibrated upon manufacture, but two calibration checks are made both before and after a sample is taken. The device is set to calibrate at 35 microgrammes of alcohol per 100 millilitres of breath, but the permitted range is from 32 to 37. If the first calibration check is outside the permitted range the device will abort. If the second calibration check is outside the range the device will be considered unreliable and the officer will be entitled to require blood or urine as an alternative to breath.

Before a sample is taken, the device will purge itself of any residual alcohol. At the end of the sequence, the device will produce a printout showing the result of the sample, the result of the calibration test and the result of the purging.

The Camic Breath Analyser

The basic operating principle of the Camic Breath Analyser is the same as the Lion. It also works on the basis of infra-red light absorption, but there are certain differences. In the Camic:
- the wave length is set at 3.4 microns;
- a lamp indicates when the user should begin and end providing breath samples. The sequence is normally set at six seconds;
- as many attempts as are necessary to provide a six second sample may be made within three minutes;
- the device is set to calibrate at 35 microgrammes but the permitted range is 32 to 38;
- the manufacturers claim that narrow band optical filters provide very high discrimination against possible interference from such substances as acetone.

Chapter 14

Penalties

In this chapter we shall consider:
- sentences available to the court;
- fixed penalty notices;
- endorsement and penalty points;
- disqualification;
- special reasons;
- mitigation.

Penalties Available to the Court

Imprisonment

If you are charged with an offence for which you could be imprisoned (see the list on page 131), you should seek the advice of a solicitor. Legal aid may be available to you.

It is a basic principle that a court must not pass a prison sentence unless the offence is so serious that only such a sentence can be justified; or, in the case of a violent or sexual offence, only a prison sentence would be adequate to protect the public from serious harm from the offender. This book does not, of course, deal with sexual offences, but dangerous driving and causing death by dangerous driving may be regarded as violent offences.

Before passing a prison sentence, the court is normally obliged to obtain and consider a "pre-sentence report" on the offender's background and attitude to the offence. Pre-sentence reports are prepared by probation officers on the basis of an interview or interviews with the offender.

Community Sentences

The most common community sentences, in the case of an adult, are a community service order, a probation order, and a "combination order".

The basic principle is that such a sentence may be passed only if the offence is serious enough to warrant it.

Community Service Order

This is an order requiring an offender aged sixteen or over to carry out unpaid work in the community. The order must normally be completed within twelve months of its imposition and the work is usually carried out at weekends. The nature of the work depends on the needs of the locality, but is often of a practical nature, such as painting and decorating a retirement home or community centre. The minimum number of hours that may be ordered is 40, and the maximum, 240. The length of a community service order should reflect the seriousness of the offence.

A community service order may be made only with the consent of the offender.

Probation Order

A probation order may be made in respect of any offence committed by an offender aged sixteen or over. It requires the offender to be under the supervision of a probation officer for the period of the order. It may have other conditions attached, such as attendance at an alcohol rehabilitation centre or hospital. The purpose of a probation order is to rehabilitate the offender, protect the public from harm, and prevent the commission of further offences.

A probation order may be made only with the consent of the offender.

Combination Order

This combines a community service and probation order in the same sentence.

Absolute and Conditional Discharges

Discharges may be ordered when punishment is inexpedient having regard to the nature of the offence and the character of the offender.

The condition attached to a conditional discharge is that the offender does not re-offend during the period of the order (usually two years but up to a maximum of three years). If the offender does re-offend during the period of the discharge, the offender may be sentenced for the original offence in any way that he or she could have been sentenced immediately following conviction for that offence.

An absolute discharge is without conditions, and is appropriate where there is no moral blame to be attached to the offender, for example, where a motorist used a vehicle without insurance, but had paid the premium to a broker who failed to pass it on to the insurance company.

Fines

The fine accounts for 86 per cent of all sentences imposed by magistrates' courts for road traffic offences. The Crown Court may impose fines of an unlimited amount, but the magistrates' court is restricted to certain maxima depending on the gravity of the offence. Throughout the text you will see references to different levels. They have been explained earlier, but for the sake of convenience, the maximum fines for each level are set out again here:

Level 1:	£200
Level 2:	£500
Level 3:	£1,000
Level 4:	£2,500
Level 5:	£5,000.

Before determining the amount of a fine, the court must inquire into the financial circumstances of the offender. Most courts have pre-printed forms on which defendants can set out their income and outgoings. The court is empowered to make a "financial circumstances order" – an order requiring the offender to give to the court a statement of his or her financial circumstances. If the offender fails to do so (or fails to provide sufficient information) the court may make such order as it thinks fit. In practice, this means that the court will impose a heavier fine than might have been the case if the offender had complied with the order. The amount of the fine must reflect the court's opinion of the seriousness of the offence.

Strictly, fines are payable immediately they are imposed. In practice, the court will usually allow time to pay, either by instalments or by fixing a date by which the total amount must be paid. It is up to the offender to ask for time to pay. The court will have inquired into the offender's financial circumstances and will therefore expect a realistic offer of payment by instalments or by a certain date.

If you are fined at a magistrates' court outside the area in which you live, the court may make a "transfer of fine" order. This means that the fine will be registered at and payable to your local magistrates' court.

If you fall behind with payments, and in particular if your financial circumstances deteriorate after the fine was imposed, it is wise to contact the court to explain what has happened. If you fail to pay and give no explanation, the court may issue a warrant for your arrest. If the court finds that you failed to pay because of "wilful refusal" or "culpable neglect", it is empowered to impose a prison sentence.

Fixed Penalty Notices

A fixed penalty notice is a notice offering a motorist the opportunity to avoid conviction by paying a fixed penalty. If you have the opportunity to pay a fixed penalty and do not dispute the matter, it is advisable to pay the fixed penalty. This is because the fixed penalty will almost certainly be lower than a fine imposed by a magistrates' court, and there will be no order for costs.

The present levels of fixed penalties are as follows:
– for offences leading to obligatory endorsement, £40;
– for illegal parking on a red route, £40;
– for illegal parking in London (other than on a red route), £30;
– for illegal parking elsewhere and non-endorsable offences, £20.

A list of the offences which can be dealt with by a fixed penalty notice is given on page 132.

The Procedure

When a fixed penalty is issued, proceedings will not be brought until the end of what is known as the "suspended enforcement period". The suspended enforcement period is 21 days, or longer if specified in the notice, although in practice it is 28 days.

There is a presumption that the keeper of the vehicle at the time of of the offence was the owner.

If no response is received by the end of the suspended enforcement period, the police may serve a "notice to owner". The notice will give particulars of the alleged offence and of the fixed penalty, and state the period allowed to respond to the notice.

The person upon whom the notice is served should, if appropriate, and within the time specified in the notice to owner, forward to the police a "statutory notice of ownership". This notice should state whether or not the person owned the vehicle at the time of the offence, and if not, (a) whether the person was never the owner; or (b) that ownership ceased before or commenced after the time of the alleged offence. It should also give such details as are known about the present owner.

The procedure differs according to whether the offence is endorsable or non-endorsable, and whether the notice was given personally to the driver or fixed to the vehicle. A list of endorsable offences is set out on pages 131 to 132. If the person who receives a notice steadfastly ignores it, eventually the matter will be registered as a fine at court, and the court will take steps to recover the money.

There is also a procedure for conditional fixed penalties where the fixed penalty notice for an endorsable offence is not given personally to the driver.

Endorsable Offences

A constable in uniform (but not a traffic warden) who has reason to believe that a person is committing or has committed a fixed penalty offence may give the person a fixed penalty notice.

Because the offence is endorsable, the person must produce a driving licence so that it can be checked to see whether the person is liable for disqualification under the "totting up" provisions (see page 127). If the driver cannot produce his or her driving licence at the time, the constable may issue a notice for it to be produced within seven days (see page 15). The licence will then be checked at the police station to see whether the person is liable to disqualification under the "totting up" provisions.

If the person is a "totter", no further action under the fixed penalty procedure will be taken. The case will instead proceed to court where the question of disqualification will be dealt with.

If the person is not a "totter", then the officer at the police station issues a fixed penalty notice.

Non-endorsable Offences

A constable who has reason to believe that a non-endorsable fixed penalty offence is being committed or has been committed in respect of a stationary vehicle, may fix a fixed penalty notice to that vehicle.

The fixed penalty notice must give particulars of the alleged offence, the amount of the fixed penalty, and the address of the court to which the fixed penalty may be sent.

Proceedings will not be brought until the end of the suspended enforcement period.

Responding to a Fixed Penalty Notice

Notice Given Personally

If the fixed penalty notice was given to a motorist in person, and the motorist pays the fixed penalty before the end of the suspended enforcement period, no proceedings may be brought.

If the motorist disputes that an offence was committed, he or she should, before the end of the suspended enforcement period, request a hearing. The case will then be tried by the magistrates' court.

If the person who received the notice does nothing before the end of the suspended enforcement period, the police may register a sum equal to the fixed penalty, plus one half, as a fine. This means that failure to pay may lead to the same consequences as failing to pay a fine imposed by the court (see page 121). Where a fixed penalty is registered as a fine, the magistrates' court must give notice of the registration to the alleged defaulter. If that persons claims not to be the person who was given the fixed penalty notice, or, before the end of the suspended enforcement period, requests a court hearing, he or she may make a statutory declaration (see page 25) to that effect.

Notice fixed to Vehicle

If the fixed penalty notice was fixed to the vehicle rather than given to the motorist in person, no proceedings may be brought if the amount is paid before the end of the suspended enforcement period. If the person who received the notice disputes that an offence was committed, he or she should, before the end of the suspended enforcement period, request a hearing. The case will then be tried at the magistrates' court.

If the person does nothing before the end of the suspended

enforcement period, the procedure is different in that the police then send a "notice to owner". This provides an opportunity for the recipient to explain that he or she was not responsible for the vehicle at the time (see above, page 122). Alternatively, at this stage, the owner may pay the fixed penalty within the time allowed and no proceedings may be brought. But if there is no response, the police may register the fixed penalty as a fine.

Where a fixed penalty is registered as a fine, the magistrates' court must give notice of the registration to the alleged defaulter. In the case of a notice affixed to the vehicle, if the alleged defaulter:
- claims not to have known of the fixed penalty, fixed penalty notice or notice to owner until notice of registration of the fine was received; or
- claims not to have been the owner of the vehicle at the time of the alleged offence or to have reasonable grounds for failing to comply with the notice; or
- requested a hearing before the end of the suspended enforcement period,

the alleged defaulter may make a statutory declaration (see page 25) to that effect.

Conditional Fixed Penalties

Conditional fixed penalties were introduced to cover situations where an offence such as speeding or failing to comply with a traffic light is detected by automatic camera so that it is not possible to hand the driver a fixed penalty notice or fix it to the vehicle. The notice is sent to the registered owner.

A conditional fixed penalty notice must state:
- particulars of the alleged offence;
- the amount of the fixed penalty;
- that proceedings cannot be commenced until the end of 28 days or longer if specified;
- that if the alleged offender pays the fixed penalty (and, if the offence is endorsable, sends his or her licence), any liability to conviction will be discharged.

Where payment is made in accordance with a fixed penalty offer, no proceedings may be brought.

If there is no response, or if the conditional fixed penalty relates to an endorsable offence and the person is liable to disqualification for totting, the official responsible for fixed penalty notices must notify the police. The police will then issue a summons requiring the person to attend court. If the recipient of a conditional fixed penalty disputes that an offence was committed, he or she should, before the end of the suspended enforcement period, request a court hearing.

Endorsement and the Penalty Points System

Meaning of Endorsement

Most of the offences considered in this book are endorsable offences, and a list of endorsable offences is given on page 131. When an offence is endorsable, this means that a person convicted of it must have his or her licence marked with the particulars of the offence, including the date it was committed; the date of conviction; and the number of penalty points imposed. Endorsement must be ordered for offences carrying obligatory disqualification where the court finds special reasons for not disqualifying.

The only cases in which an offender's licence will not be endorsed for an endorsable offence are:
- where the court finds special reasons for not endorsing (see page 128); or
- where the court imposes disqualification (see page 126).

An offender convicted of an endorsable offence must produce his or her licence to the court. The court will notify the Driver and Vehicle Licensing Authority so that the endorsement may be recorded there.

More than One Offence is Committed on the Same Occasion

The general rule is that where an offender commits more than one endorsable offence on the same occasion, only the offence attracting the greatest number of penalty points will result in endorsement. However, the court does have a discretion to apply separate penalty points for each endorsable offence committed on the same occasion. This might make the offender liable to disqualification as a "totter" if twelve or more points are accumulated. For example, a person convicted of both speeding and driving without insurance may be liable to six points for speeding and eight points for no insurance, and therefore be liable for disqualification.

Disqualification

A driver may be disqualified for one of three reasons:
- after conviction for an offence carrying obligatory disqualification;
- after conviction for an offence carrying discretionary disqualification;
- as a "totter".

Obligatory Disqualification

Offences leading to obligatory disqualification carry a minimum disqualification of twelve months. This is increased to two years for manslaughter, causing death by dangerous driving or causing death by careless driving when under the influence of drink or drugs.

The minimum period is also two years where the person has committed an offence carrying obligatory disqualification and has been disqualified at least twice before, for at least 56 days, in the three years before the commission of the present offence.

Disqualification Until Test is Passed

An order for disqualification until a test is passed must be made for the following offences:
- manslaughter;
- dangerous driving;
- causing death by dangerous driving.

In such cases the offender must pass an "extended driving test" before holding a licence again.

An order for disqualification until a test is passed may also be made for any other offence involving obligatory endorsement. In such cases the offender must take an ordinary driving test before holding a licence again. The law requires a court which is considering the exercise of this power to have regard to the safety of other road users. The power must not therefore be used in a punitive way.

Discretionary Disqualification

The court has power, in respect of all other endorsable offences, to order disqualification if it decides that this is appropriate. If will normally be appropriate only in cases of bad driving, persistent motoring offences or the use of vehicles for the purposes of crime.

Penalty Points Disqualification or "Totting"

An offender who acquires twelve or more penalty points within three years is liable to disqualification as a "totter".

The system works as follows. The court imposes the appropriate number of points for the present offence. It then examines the licence to see how many points were imposed in the relevant time period. The relevant time is three years, running from the date of commission of the present offence back to the date of the commission of any previous offences.

If, including the points imposed for the present offence, the number of penalty points over the three year period totals twelve or more, the offender must be disqualified for at least six months unless there are mitigating circumstances (see page 130).

Increased Period of Disqualification

If there has been a previous disqualification within the three years before the present offence, the minimum period of disqualification is twelve months.

If there have been two previous disqualifications within three years before the present offence, the minimum period of disqualification is two years.

The Effect of a Penalty Points Disqualification

A penalty points disqualification will wipe the slate clean. This means that all points on the licence will be removed. However, where a person is disqualified for a specific offence, rather than by "totting", the penalty points stay on the licence.

Mitigating Circumstances

The court has a discretion not to impose a penalty points disqualification, or to impose a shorter period of disqualification than would otherwise be appropriate, where it is satisfied that there are grounds for "mitigating" (or reducing) the normal consequences of

conviction. Grounds for mitigating do not include:
- any circumstances that are alleged to make the offence not serious;
- hardship unless it is exceptional hardship;
- any circumstances which have been taken into account as mitigating circumstances leading to non-disqualification or a shorter period of disqualification within the three years before the present conviction.

By far the most commonly argued of these is exceptional hardship. There is no legal definition of "exceptional" but it is clear that it must relate to something over and above the normal consequences of disqualification. Examples will be:
- loss of employment;
- loss of employment to others where an employer is disqualified;
- exceptional hardship to other family members, for example, inability to take children to school particularly where no other form of transport is available, such as in a rural area; or inability to visit and care for an elderly parent.

It should be noted that these are examples only and much will depend on the plausibility of the offender and the individual circumstances of the case.

Interim Disqualification

Where a case is adjourned after a person has been convicted of an offence involving obligatory or discretionary disqualification, but sentence has not been imposed, the court may order the offender to be disqualified until sentence is passed.

A case may be adjourned after conviction but before sentence in order to obtain a DVLA printout or a pre-sentence report.

An interim disqualification reduces the overall length of the period of disqualification imposed when the offender is sentenced.

Special Reasons

A court may refrain from disqualifying in cases subject to obligatory disqualification, or from endorsing for an endorsable offence, if it finds special reasons for not disqualifying or endorsing. For special reasons in the context of alcohol-related offences, see page 110.

A special reason must be a mitigating or extenuating circumstance;

it must not amount in law to a defence. It must be directly connected to the commission of the offence and it must be a matter which the court ought properly to take into account when considering sentence. This is best explained by looking at some decided cases:

Careless or dangerous driving

— An ambulance driver ignored a red traffic light while taking an emergency case to hospital. He caused the death of a motor cyclist and was convicted of causing death by dangerous driving. He was given an absolute discharge and the court found special reasons for not disqualifying.
— A police officer on a training exercise ignored a red traffic light and was convicted of careless driving. The court did not find special reasons for not endorsing because the offender was on a training exercise and not in a situation of real emergency.
— A police officer responding to an emergency call was convicted of careless driving. The court found special reasons for not endorsing.

Speeding

— A trainee solicitor was caught speeding on his way to court. It was held that there were special reasons for not endorsing.
— A solicitor on his way to an emergency meeting with a client exceeded the motorway speed limit over a long stretch of road because he heard on the radio that snow was forecast and he wanted to get off the motorway quickly. The court did not find special reasons for not endorsing his licence.
— A 40 m.p.h. stretch of road changed to a 30 m.p.h. stretch but there was no speed limit notice. A driver who continued to drive at 40 m.p.h. was convicted of exceeding the speed limit, but the court found special reasons for not endorsing.

Using Without Insurance

The court will find special reasons for not endorsing only where the offender was misled into committing the offence, either by another person or by a lack of clarity in the policy. There must have been some element of misleading and not ignorance alone, for example, where a driver of a borrowed vehicle was assured by the owner that the owner's policy covered drivers using the vehicle with the owner's permission, but this turned out not to be the case.

Traffic Signs

The court will find special reasons for not endorsing only where there was an emergency and the driving did not endanger other road users. In a decided case, special reasons were found where a driver performed a U-turn across the central reservation of a motorway when the carriageway in which the driver was travelling was blocked by traffic, but the opposite carriageway was empty. This decision turned on its own facts and should not be considered as authorisation for undertaking U-turns on motorways.

Mitigation

The term "mitigation" is much wider than mitigating circumstances or special reasons. Few offenders will have mitigating circumstances if they have acquired 12 penalty points in three years. Few will have special reasons, but everyone will have mitigation.

Mitigation refers to:
- the circumstances of the offence; for example, explaining why it was committed; cooperation with the police following the event; or responsible behaviour such as calling the emergency services after an accident;
- the personal circumstances of the offender. These will include a good driving record; a high number of miles travelled each year without offence; a good work record; military service; charitable work; and family circumstances.

Mitigation may also include unfortunate circumstances, such as a pending divorce, loss of employment, bad health and a recent bereavement.

For guidance on how to write a letter in mitigation, see page 31.

Perhaps the most important feature of mitigation is a timely plea of guilty which will normally result in a discount of one third off the appropriate sentence.

Penalties

List of Imprisonable Offences

- Dangerous driving
- Manslaughter
- Causing death by dangerous driving
- Careless driving whilst under the influence of drink or drugs
- Driving or attempting to drive with excess alcohol
- Driving or attempting to drive whilst unfit
- Failing to provide an evidential specimen
- In charge whilst unfit or with excess alcohol
- Taking without consent
- Allowing oneself to be carried in a taken vehicle
- Aggravated vehicle taking
- Interfering with a motor vehicle
- Failing to stop after or report an accident
- Causing danger to road users
- Driving whilst disqualified
- Driving after refusal or revocation of licence
- Wanton and furious driving
- Fraudulent use of an excise licence

List of Endorsable Offences

- Contravention of a temporary prohibition or restriction
- Breach of motorway regulations other than walking on a motorway
- Breach of pedestrian crossing regulations
- Failing to stop at a school crossing
- Contravention of an order relating to street playgrounds
- Exceeding the speed limit
- Causing death by dangerous driving
- Dangerous driving
- Careless and inconsiderate driving
- Causing death by careless driving when under the influence of drink or drugs
- Driving or attempting to drive when unfit through drink or drugs
- In charge of a mechanically propelled vehicle when unfit to drive through drink or drugs
- Driving or attempting to drive with excess alcohol
- Being in charge of a motor vehicle with excess alcohol

Penalties

- Failing to provide a specimen for a breath test
- Failing to provide a specimen for analysis or laboratory test
- Motor racing and speed trials on a public way
- Leaving a vehicle in a dangerous position
- Carrying a passenger on a motor cycle
- Failing to comply with a traffic direction
- Failing to comply with a traffic sign
- Leaving a vehicle in a dangerous position
- Breach of requirement as to brakes, steering gear or tyres
- Driving otherwise than in accordance with a driving licence
- Driving after making a false declaration as to fitness
- Driving after failing to notify a relevant or prospective disability
- Driving with uncorrected defective eyesight or refusing to submit to an eyesight test
- Driving whilst disqualified
- Uninsured use of a motor vehicle
- Failing to stop after an accident or report an accident.

List of Offences Leading to Obligatory Disqualification

- Causing death by careless driving when under the influence of drink or drugs
- Dangerous driving
- Causing death by dangerous driving
- Driving or attempting to drive when unfit through drink or drugs
- Driving or attempting to drive with excess alcohol
- Failing to provide a specimen for analysis when driving or attempting to drive
- Racing and speed trials on a public way
- Motor manslaughter.

List of Fixed Penalty Offences

- Using or keeping a vehicle on a public road without exhibiting a licence in the prescribed manner
- Driving or keeping a vehicle without the required registration mark or hackney carriage sign
- Driving or keeping a vehicle with the registration mark or hackney carriage sign obscured

Penalties

- Parking a vehicle on the footway or verge in Greater London
- Obstructing the highway where the offence is committed by a vehicle
- Using a vehicle in contravention of a traffic regulation order outside Greater London
- Breach of traffic regulation order within Greater London
- Breach of experimental traffic order
- Breach of experimental traffic scheme regulations in Greater London
- Using a vehicle in contravention of a temporary prohibition or restriction of traffic
- Wrongful use of motorway
- Using a motor vehicle in contravention of a provision for one-way traffic on a trunk road
- Driving a vehicle in contravention of an order prohibiting or restricting the driving of vehicles on certain classes of road
- Breach of certain pedestrian crossing regulations
- Using a vehicle in contravention of a street playground order
- Breach of certain orders regulating the use of parking places provided by a local authority
- Using a vehicle in contravention of any provision of a parking place designation order
- Contravention of a minimum speed limit
- Speeding offences
- Breach of seat belt regulations
- Breach of restriction on carrying children in the front of a vehicle
- Breach of restriction on carrying children in the rear of a vehicle
- Breach of regulations relating to protective head gear
- Parking heavy commercial vehicle on a verge or footway
- Parking a vehicle other than a heavy commercial vehicle on a verge or footway
- Leaving a vehicle in a dangerous position
- Unlawful carrying of passengers on motor cycles
- Driving a motor vehicle elsewhere than on a road
- Failing to comply with traffic directions
- Failing to comply with a traffic sign
- Using a vehicle in a dangerous condition

- Breach of requirements as to brakes, steering gear or tyres
- Breach of requirement as to weight
- Breach of other construction and use regulations
- Driving a vehicle otherwise than in accordance with a licence
- Failing to stop a vehicle on being so required by a constable in uniform.

Index

Absolute discharge, 119–120
Accident(s), 67–69
    breath tests following,
        101–102
    meaning of, 18
    reporting, 67
    stopping after, 67
Adjournment notice, 21
Aggravated vehicle taking, 91–92
Alcohol:
    driving or attempting to drive
        with excess, 102–106, 113
    drugs and, 97–117
    effect of on dangerous driving, 47
    effects of, 97–99
Alternative verdict, 48, 49
Animals on a motorway, 60
Arrest, powers of, 14, 100
Arrestable offence, 22
Attempting to drive:
    excess alcohol, with, 102–106,
        113
    meaning of, 17
Attention, driving without due care
    and, 43–44

Blood specimens, 104–106
Brakes, 65
Breath:
    analysis machines, operating
        principles of, 116–117
    tests, 103-104, 116–117

    failure to provide, 103
Breathalyser, 101–102

Camera, offences caught on,
    124–125
Camic breath analyser, 117
Care and attention, driving without
    due, 43–44
Careless driving, causing death by
    when under the influence of drink
    or drugs, 112–113, 114–115
Careless or dangerous driving, 129
Carriageway:
    meaning of, 57
    not driving on, 57
Causing danger to road users, 95–96
"Causing or permitting", meaning of,
    19
Central reservation, 57, 59
Charge, 21
Charge, in, whilst unfit or with
    excess alcohol, 107–108, 113
Children, wearing of seat belts by,
    79–80
Class(es) of vehicle, 18–19
    exceeding the speed limit
        applicable to, 54
    excluded from motorways, 60
Clerk to the court, 27
Combination order, 189
Community sentences, 118–119
Community Service Order, 119

Index

Compensation, 26–27
Condition of a vehicle, 62–66
Conditional:
  discharge, 119–120
  fixed penalty, 124–125
Consideration, driving without reasonable, 45
Construction and use of vehicles, 62–66
"Conveyance":
  meaning of, 89
  taking, 88–91
Conviction, 23
Corroboration, 23
Costs, 26
Court procedure, 27–35
Crash helmets, 80–81
Criminal offences, 88–96
Cross-examination, 25
Crown Prosecution Service, 28

Danger, causing, to other road users, 95–96
Dangerous:
  condition, vehicle in, 62
  driving, 45–49
  position, vehicle in, 86
Death:
  careless driving, by, when under the influence of drink or drugs, 112–113, 114–115
  dangerous driving, by, 48–49
Detention, powers of, 14
Disabled persons, parking concessions for, 83
Discharge, 119–120
Disqualification, 126–130
  accumulating penalty points, for, 127
  application for driving licence after, 94
  drink driving, for, 110–112
  discretionary, 126–127
  interim, 128–129
  obligatory, 126, 132
  removal of or reduction of period of, 115–116
  special reasons for not, 128–130
Disqualified:
  driving whilst, 93–94
  obtaining a driving licence while, 94
Documents, 36–42
  failing to produce, 37
  power to require production of, 15
Door of vehicle, opening, 86–87
Drink-driving, 97–117
Driver, identity of, 15–16
Driving:
  disqualified, whilst, 93–94
  due care and attention, without, 43–44
  excess alcohol, with, 102–106, 113
  meaning of, 17
  reasonable consideration, without, 45
  unfit, whilst, 106–107, 113
  wanton or furious, 50
Driving licence:
  applying for after disqualification, 94
  driving after refusal or revocation of, 40–41
  driving otherwise than in accordance with, 39–40
  obtaining, while disqualified, 94
Drugs, 97–117
Due care and attention, driving without, 43–44
Duty solicitor, 15, 28
DVLA, 19

Index

"Either way" offence, 22
Emergency services, exemption from
    speed limits for, 55
Endorsable offences, 131–132
    fixed penalty procedure for,
        122–125
    parking, 85–86
Endorsement, 125–126
Entry, powers of, 101
"Entry point", meaning of, 26
Evidence, 23
    giving, 33–35
    impairment of ability to drive, of,
        107
    speeding cases, in, 55
Examination in chief, 24
Excess alcohol:
    driving or attempting to drive
        with, 102–106, 113
    in charge with 107–108, 113
Excise licence:
    failing to display, 42
    fraudulent use of, 94–95
    using or keeping a vehicle
        without, 41–42

Failing:
    comply with a traffic sign, to,
        70–73
    produce documents, to, 37
    provide a specimen, to, 108–110,
        114
    report an accident, to, 67
    stop after an accident, to, 67
Financial means of offender,
    120–121
Fines, 120–121
Fingerprints, 88
Fixed penalty:
    notices, 23, 121–125
    offences, list of, 132–134
Forfeiture, 27

Furious or wanton driving, 50

Give way signs, failure to comply
    with, 72
Guilty plea, 25, 30–33

Hard shoulder, 57, 59
Highway, obstruction of, 85–86
Highway Code, 44
Hospital patients, protection for, 99,
    108

Impairment of ability to drive,
    106–107
Imprisonable offences, 131
Imprisonment, 118
In charge whilst unfit or with excess
    alcohol, 107–108, 113
Inconvenience to other road users, 45
Indictable offence, 22
Insurance :
    certificate, failing to produce, 37,
        68
    using without, 37–38, 129–130
Interfering with a motor vehicle,
    92–93
Interim disqualification, 128

"Joy riding", 88–92

Laced drinks, 112
Learner drivers, 39–40, 59
Letter, pleading guilty by, 31–32
Limits of alcohol, 102–103
Lion Intoximeter, 116–117
Loading and unloading, 83
Loads, 64
Local:
    speed limits, 54
    parking restrictions, 82–83

Magistrates' courts, 27–35

Index

Magistrates, 27
Means of offender, 120–121
Mechanical defect, incident caused by, 44, 46
Mechanically propelled vehicle, meaning of, 18
Medical condition:
    leading to refusal or revocation of driving licence, 40–41
    preventing giving breath specimen, 109
Mitigation, 26, 31–32, 33, 127–128, 130
Mobile telephones, 44
Motor:
    cycle, meaning of, 17
    manslaughter, 49–50
    racing, 50
    vehicle, meaning of, 17
Motoring offences distinguished from criminal offences, 88
Motorway, 57–61
    speeding on, 55

"No waiting" areas, 82–83
Non-endorsable:
    offence, fixed penalty for, 125
    parking offences, 84–85
Not guilty, pleading, 33–35
"Notice to owner", 84, 121–122

Obstruction of the highway, 85–86
Offences, 21–22, 88
    lists of, 131–134
Offender, means of, 120–121
Opening vehicle door, 86–87
Overtaking:
    zebra-controlled area, in, 75, 77

Parking, 82–87
    meters, 82
    tickets, 84–85

Passengers, 63
Pedestrian crossing, 74–77
Pedestrians, walking on a motorway, 60
Pelican crossing:
    failure to afford precedence on, 76
    identification of, 74–75
    stopping in area adjacent to, 76
Penalties, 118–134
    range of, 118–121
    standard scale of, 26, 120
Penalty:
    charge notices, 84–95
    points, 125–128
"Permitting" an offence, 19, 90
Plea, 24
Pleading guilty, 30–33
Police powers, 13–16, 88, 99–102
Preliminary breath test, 101–102
"Printout", 19
Probation order, 119
Procedure:
    court, in, 27–35
    fixed penalties, for 121–125
Producing documents, 36–37
Prohibition notice, 15
Proof, 24
Prosecutor, 27, 34
Protective headgear, 80–81
Public place, meaning of, 18
Purpose for which vehicle is used, 63

Racing, 50
Rear seat belts, 80
Reasonable consideration, driving without, 45
Reduction of period of disqualification, 115–116
Removal:
    disqualification, of, 115–116
    vehicles, of, 16

Index

Report an accident, failing to, 67
Restricted road:
    exceeding the speed limit on, 52–53
    meaning of, 52–53
Reversing on a motorway, 59
Right hand lane, 59–60
Road:
    checks, 13
    meaning of, 18
    users, causing danger to, 95–96
Road fund licence:
    failing to display, 42
    fraudulent use of, 94–95
    using or keeping a vehicle without, 41–42
Roadside breath test, 101–102

Screening test, 101–102
Seat belts, 78–80
    exemption from wearing, 78–79
Serious arrestable offence, 22
Special reasons for not disqualifying, 110–112, 128–130
Specimen:
    failing to provide, 108–110, 114
    private testing of, 105–106
Speeding, 52–56, 129
Standard scale of penalties, 26, 120
Statement, 24
Statutory declaration, 25
"Statutory notice of ownership", 122
Steering, 65
Stop:
    failing to after an accident, 67
    motorway, on, 58
    pedestrian crossing, on or near, 75, 76
    search, and, power to, 13
    sign, failure to comply with, 72
Street lighting, 52–53

Strict liability, 22, 65, 93
Summary offence, 22
Summons, 20–21, 28–30

Taking :
    a conveyance, 88–91
    without consent, 88–92
Tax disc:
    failing to display, 42
    fraudulent use of, 94–95
    using or keeping a vehicle without, 41–42
Temporary speed limit, 53–54
Temporary speed restriction, 53–54
Terminology, 16–27
Test certificate, 38–39
Test, disqualification until passed, 126
"Tickets" – see fixed penalty notices
"Totter", 25, 127
Traffic:
    directions, 70
    lights, failure to comply with, 71
    signs, 70–73, 130
Trial, 23, 33–35
Tyres, 64–65

U-turns, 58
Unfit:
    driving whilst, 106–107, 113
    in charge whilst, 107–108, 113
Uninsured vehicle, 37–38, 129–130
Unloading, 83
Urine specimens, 104–106
Use, construction and, of vehicles, 62–66
Usher, 28

Vehicle:
    class, exceeding the speed limit applicable to, 54
    classes of, 18–19

construction and use of, 62–66
   defect rectification scheme, 19, 66
   interfering with, 92–93
   purpose for which used, 63
   taking, aggravated, 91–92
Verdict, 23, 48, 49
Verge, motorway, of, 57, 59

Wanton or furious driving, 50
Warning formula, 20
Wheel clamping, 83–84
White lines, failure to comply with, 72
"Widmark formula", 106
Witness(es), 34, 35
Written statement, proof by, 24
Wrong direction, driving in, 58

Zebra crossing:
   failure to afford precedence on, 75, 76
   identification of, 74
Zebra-controlled area:
   overtaking in, 75
   stopping in, 75